DRAWING HOME PLANS

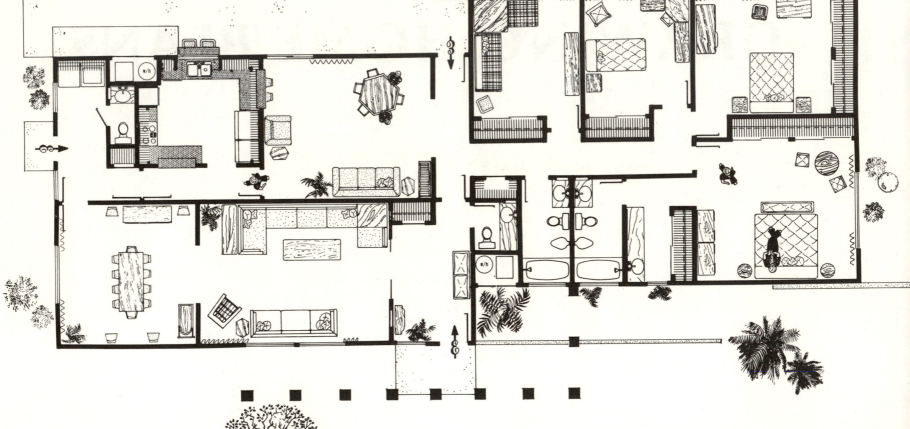

DRAWING HOME PLANS

A SIMPLIFIED DRAFTING SYSTEM FOR PLANNING AND DESIGN

JUNE CURRAN

Registered Building Designer
Member American Institute of Building Design

Designs and Illustrations by the Author

BROOKS

BROOKS PUBLISHING COMPANY
Bakersfield, California

First published in 1976 by the McGraw-Hill Book Company

Brooks Publishing Company titles are distributed worldwide by William Kaufmann, Inc., Los Altos, California. For further information regarding distribution outside of the United States of America, write to Foreign Sales Department, William Kaufmann, Inc., One First Street, Los Altos, CA 94022.

10 9 8 7 6 5 4 3 2 1

Library of Congress Cataloging in Publication Data

Curran, June,
    Drawing home plans.

    Published in 1976 under title: Drawing plans for your own home.

    Includes bibliographical references and index.
    1. Architecture, Domestic—Designs and plans.
    2. Architectural drawing—Technique. I. Title.
NA7115.C87 1979   728.3   78-72188

ISBN 0-932370-01-2
ISBN 0-932370-02-0 pbk.   Printed in the United States of America by Malloy Lithographing, Inc.

DEDICATED TO BETTER HOUSING
FOR EVERYONE, EVERYWHERE.

ACKNOWLEDGEMENTS

I have been so fortunate, during the critical stages of editing this new edition of "Drawing Home Plans," to have had encouragement and support from my husband, Hugh Curran; the editing skills of my assistant, Nancy Giumarra; and copy editing help from Alice Gosak.

My daughter, Shay Wilbur, devoted long hours to manuscript typing; and my friend, Evanell Yelich enhanced my illustrations with her skillful lettering.

I would like to thank all those at Hoven & Co., Inc. who contributed, particularly Estelle Wolf who operates the magical typesetting machine, and Eileen Raborg who was responsible for much of the page composition.

FOREWORD

In a time when the normal has become "unduly complexed," it is refreshing indeed to see a work that is of "superior simplicity." I enjoyed very much seeing the approach to spelling out in a simplified fashion the true objective of each sub-heading of the drawing plans system. It has been my past experience that most people think of planning (designing), and the imparting of their creative thoughts to paper as being complicated and forbidding to the point of being reluctant to just put their thoughts down in a simple straightforward fashion. I believe that this fear of graphically imparting thoughts must come from past instructions and complexed textbooks; and of course, one's natural fear of putting something into written form that isn't automatically beautiful to start with.

I feel that this type of simplified, technically illustrated book, while it may seem to some to be over-simplified, would be an excellent guide for anyone 6 years to 90 years who is interested in designing homes.

I have, over the past ten years, hired some 100 plus drafters who have ranged from a student working as a summer employee to gain experience, to licensed graduate architects. Of these, I would say a full 50% could have very well benefitted from a general reading of "Drawing Home Plans." (The ability to draw is a necessary evil of designing and passing on to others information. If we could only come up with a machine that would literally take our thoughts and illustrate them graphically.)

"Drawing Home Plans" would be an excellent book for a designer to hand to the client who wants to become involved in the planning of his or her home. In other words, the client could be a real part of the design team, which in my opinion, is the ideal situation.

The theme I have tried to stress in my above comments is to applaud the author's efforts toward simplicity . . . simplicity of reading and simplicity of explanations of the desired end result.

Dave Gardner Cross, AIA
Architect

PREFACE

The intent of this book is to give you the necessary information to actually draw plans for a home. Whether you wish to plan your own home or become a design professional, you will find that this simplified system of drawing home plans will make it easy for you to design and draw plans for a remodeling project, an addition to a home, or a new home. The book will also help you to understand and read prints of house plans drawn by others. If you are dealing with a design professional, you can save his or her time and your money because you will be able to sketch your requirements and visualize the plans presented to you.

The secret of designing a home is to learn to express your thoughts accurately on paper. The information and step-by-step instructions in this book will show you how to draw ideas in accurate scale, using symbols and designations that are readily understandable to contractors, designers, craftspersons, and everyone in the construction industry.

As you follow the simplified system of analyzing needs and drawing plans presented in this book, you will find that you are soon able to visualize the entire project. Putting your ideas on paper will clarify the facts and help you to discuss requirements with others involved. Because the methods shown in the following pages are mechanical, in the sense that a hand guides a pencil against a straight-edge, anyone with a little persistence can complete any of the projects depicted, even though those in the back sections of the book may, at first glance, appear to be difficult.

If you are a person who thinks of yourself as not being creative or not having artistic talent, you will be amazed to find that you do have the ability to perceive, create, and design, which will become more apparent as you proceed with the successive projects.

June Curran

1

TABLE
OF
CONTENTS

CHAPTER FOUR
DRAWING A PLAN OF THE BUILDING SITE FOR NEW HOMES . . . ADDITIONS . . . REMODELING
PAGE 43

CHAPTER FIVE
SYMBOLS, SIZES, AND DESCRIPTIONS FOR DRAWING AND READING PLANS
PAGE 63

CHAPTER SIX
PRELIMINARY PLANNING   **PAGE 93**

CHAPTER SEVEN
DRAWING ROOM STUDIES FROM PRELIMINARY PLANS   **PAGE 101**

CHAPTER EIGHT
PLANNING VEHICLE AREAS   **PAGE 113**

CHAPTER FOURTEEN
DRAWING PLANS FOR THE EXTERIOR OF A HOME   **PAGE 161**

CHAPTER FIFTEEN
HOW TO OBTAIN A SET OF PRINTS   **PAGE 191**

CHAPTER ONE

HOW THE DRAWING PLANS SYSTEM WORKS

PROJECT 1   **Components and Equipment**

EXPRESS YOUR IDEAS ON PAPER

You can learn enough about drawing home plans from this book to be able to express your own ideas on paper. Anyone can!

Individuals who are drawing plans either for a new home, or to remodel a home, begin with a general idea of what they desire to achieve. To convert ideas to the reality of a solidly structured plan, each idea must be crystallized into a decision which becomes a fact, and this fact must be put down on paper.

HOW TO REDUCE A HOUSE TO FIT ON A PIECE OF PAPER

Since a house is a very large object, and the paper on which it is drawn must of necessity be a convenient size, a method has been devised that makes it possible to accurately draw a representation of a house that will fit on a piece of paper.

When you reduce something as large as a house to the size of a piece of paper, you must have some system for keeping spaces in correct relative proportion to each other. The method that has evolved and been perfected over the years is called **drawing in scale**. Drawing in scale means reducing a house, a lot, or an individual room to a size that will fit on a sheet of paper that can easily be handled.

Though different scales are used for various types of work, house plans are almost always drawn to a scale in which one-quarter of an inch is equal to one foot, written 1/4″ = 1′; this means that a line is drawn one-quarter of an inch long to represent each foot of actual house space. More detailed information about this is given farther along in this chapter.

PLAN DRAWING - A SIMPLE LANGUAGE OF LINES

If you were looking at a set of house plans for the first time, you might be quite confused by the great number of lines and symbols. At first glance, plans *are* confusing. However, there is a simple formula for drawing them. Think of these lines and symbols as a language of lines, used and understood by drafters and construction people who execute designs.

Whether the plan is to build a new home, remodel or add to a home, or just improve furniture arrangements within existing space, you will gain much by putting these ideas on paper. In this way you can visualize and finalize ideas and also make them clear and understandable to others.

Some of the answers you have been looking for will become clear for you when you begin to understand *how to work in scale*. Eventually, with a little practice, you will be able to visualize your entire project on paper.

PROJECT 1   Components and Equipment

Objective: *To become familiar with the drawing plans system components and other useful equipment. Learn how to create good drawing arrangements.*

Materials Required: *The drawing system components; scale rulers in three sizes, cut-out and tracing guide symbols*

THE DRAWING PLANS SYSTEM COMPONENTS

It is much easier to get started drawing if you have the proper materials and supplies to work with. For this reason, I have designed components for the simplified drafting system presented here. Included with the book are:

SCALE RULERS IN THREE SIZES

One-Quarter-Inch equals One Foot (1/4″ = 1′)
One-Eighth-Inch equals One Foot (1/8″ = 1′)
One-Sixteenth-Inch equals One Foot (1/16″ = 1′)

These rulers located on **Page 229**, should be carefully cut out with scissors.

DESIGN GUIDE SYMBOLS

The design guide symbols on the following pages represent all the component parts of a house; kitchen appliances and cabinets, plumbing fixtures, electrical outlets, fireplaces, furniture, cars, landscaping, and figures of men, women, and children in plan. Refer to **Pages 12-19**.

This same set of symbols on **Pages 215-227** can be cut out from the book, and placed on your drawing, to aid in room planning and arrangement. The symbol sheets are reproduced in one-quarter-inch scale and can be placed on a plan drawn to the same scale to help you visualize space requirements.

USING SYMBOLS AS CUT-OUTS:

1. Check sizes and select the most appropriate items for your plan.

2. Cut the items out with scissors. The paper can be cut a little smaller or larger to fit your own size requirements where necessary. (Measure with your scale ruler.)

3. Arrange the symbols on the plan to suit your space requirements.

USING SYMBOLS AS TRACING GUIDES:

1. When you are satisfied with your arrangement of the cut-out symbols, simply lay a piece of tracing paper over the page and trace the layout.

2. Slip the layout tracing under your original drawing and trace the symbols on to the plan.

The following pages contain detailed information about other equipment and supplies that will help you to produce a more professional looking drawing.

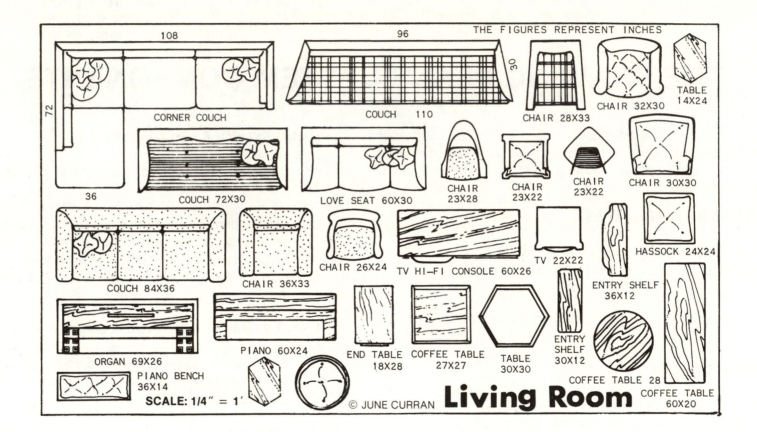

Figure 1.   Living Room design guide symbols.

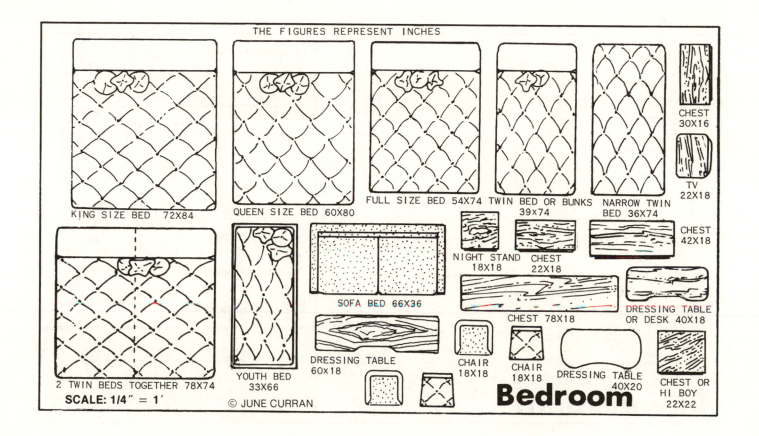

Figure 1a.   Bedroom design guide symbols.

1
3

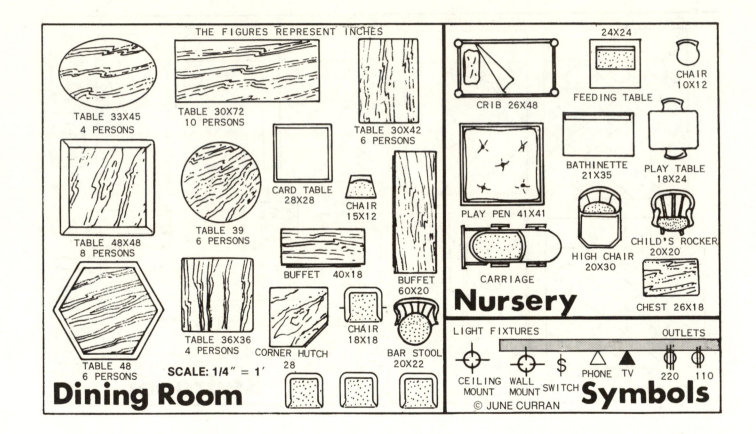

THE FIGURES REPRESENT INCHES

Dining Room

TABLE 33X45
4 PERSONS

TABLE 30X72
10 PERSONS

TABLE 30X42
6 PERSONS

CARD TABLE
28X28

CHAIR
15X12

TABLE 48X48
8 PERSONS

TABLE 39
6 PERSONS

BUFFET 40x18

BUFFET
60X20

TABLE 48
6 PERSONS

TABLE 36X36
4 PERSONS

CORNER HUTCH
28

CHAIR
18X18

BAR STOOL
20X22

SCALE: 1/4″ = 1′

Nursery

CRIB 26X48

FEEDING TABLE

24X24

CHAIR
10X12

BATHINETTE
21X35

PLAY TABLE
18X24

PLAY PEN 41X41

HIGH CHAIR
20X30

CHILD'S ROCKER
20X20

CARRIAGE

CHEST 26X18

Symbols

LIGHT FIXTURES   OUTLETS

CEILING
MOUNT

WALL
MOUNT

SWITCH

$

PHONE   TV

220   110

© JUNE CURRAN

1
4

Figure 2.   Dining Room, Nursery, and Electrical design guide symbols.

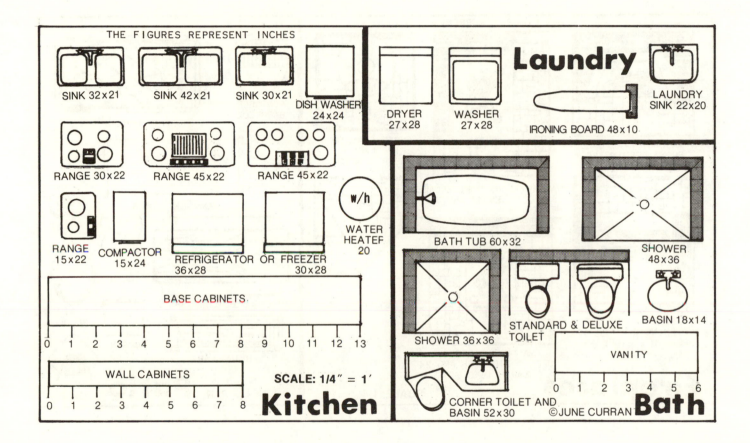

THE FIGURES REPRESENT INCHES

SINK 32x21 SINK 42x21 SINK 30x21 DISH WASHER 24x24

RANGE 30x22 RANGE 45x22 RANGE 45x22

RANGE 15x22 COMPACTOR 15x24 REFRIGERATOR 36x28 OR FREEZER 30x28 w/h WATER HEATER 20

BASE CABINETS

0 1 2 3 4 5 6 7 8 9 10 11 12 13

WALL CABINETS

0 1 2 3 4 5 6 7 8

SCALE: 1/4" = 1'

Kitchen

Laundry

DRYER 27x28 WASHER 27x28 IRONING BOARD 48x10 LAUNDRY SINK 22x20

BATH TUB 60x32 SHOWER 48x36

SHOWER 36x36 STANDARD & DELUXE TOILET BASIN 18x14

CORNER TOILET AND BASIN 52x30 ©JUNE CURRAN

VANITY

0 1 2 3 4 5 6

Bath

Figure 2a. Kitchen, Laundry, and Bath design guide symbols.

1
5

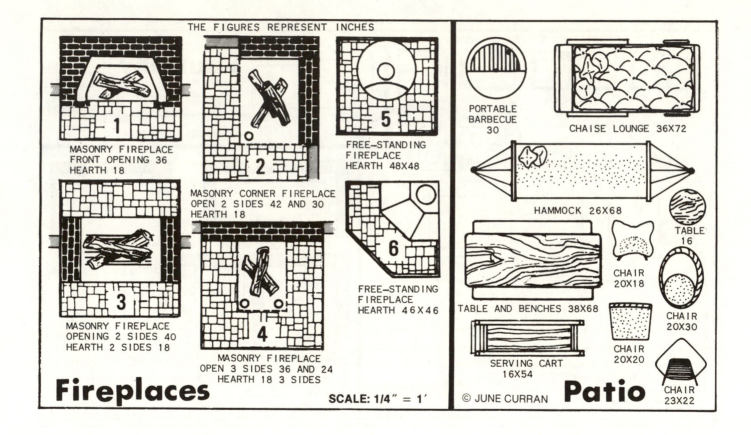

THE FIGURES REPRESENT INCHES

Fireplaces

1 — MASONRY FIREPLACE
FRONT OPENING 36
HEARTH 18

2 — MASONRY CORNER FIREPLACE
OPEN 2 SIDES 42 AND 30
HEARTH 18

3 — MASONRY FIREPLACE
OPENING 2 SIDES 40
HEARTH 2 SIDES 18

4 — MASONRY FIREPLACE
OPEN 3 SIDES 36 AND 24
HEARTH 18 3 SIDES

5 — FREE-STANDING
FIREPLACE
HEARTH 48X48

6 — FREE-STANDING
FIREPLACE
HEARTH 46X46

SCALE: 1/4″ = 1′

Patio

PORTABLE BARBECUE 30

CHAISE LOUNGE 36X72

HAMMOCK 26X68

TABLE AND BENCHES 38X68

SERVING CART 16X54

CHAIR 20X18

TABLE 16

CHAIR 20X30

CHAIR 20X20

CHAIR 23X22

© JUNE CURRAN

Figure 3.   Fireplace and Patio design guide symbols.

16

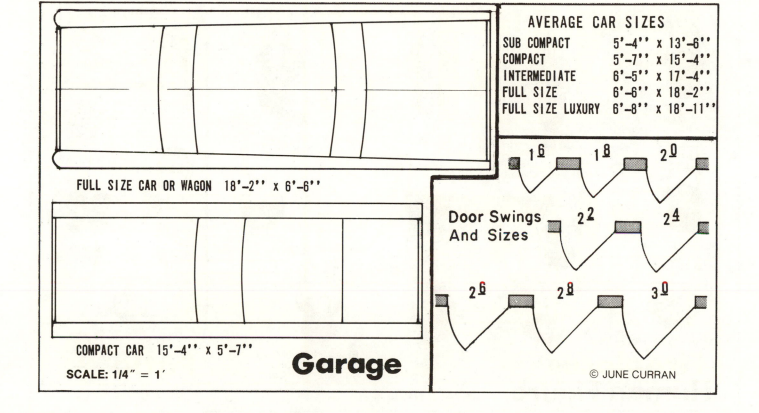

FULL SIZE CAR OR WAGON 18'-2'' x 6'-6''

COMPACT CAR 15'-4'' x 5'-7''

SCALE: 1/4" = 1'

Garage

AVERAGE CAR SIZES

SUB COMPACT	5'-4'' x 13'-6''
COMPACT	5'-7'' x 15'-4''
INTERMEDIATE	6'-5'' x 17'-4''
FULL SIZE	6'-6'' x 18'-2''
FULL SIZE LUXURY	6'-8'' x 18'-11''

Door Swings
And Sizes

16 18 20
22 24
26 28 30

© JUNE CURRAN

Figure 3a.   Garage and Door Swing Sizes design guide symbols.

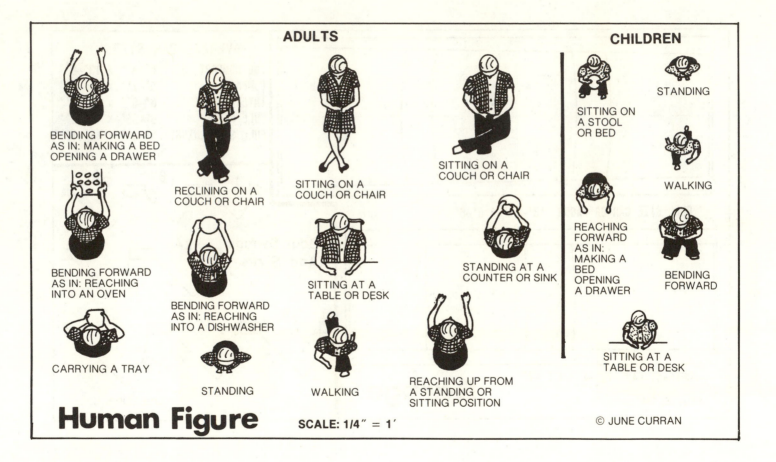

Figure 4.   Human Figure in Plan design guide symbols.

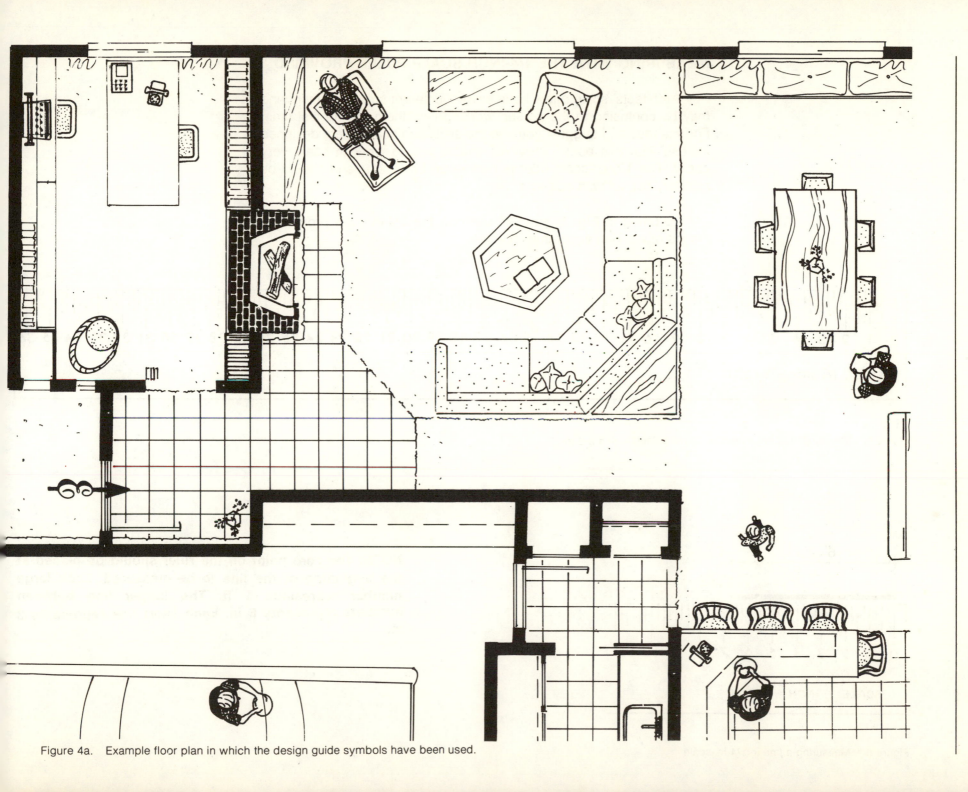

Figure 4a.   Example floor plan in which the design guide symbols have been used.

MEASURING WITH THE 1/4-INCH SCALE RULER PROVIDED

Architects' scale rulers have several different scales on them and may be confusing to the person working with them for the first time. For this reason, I suggest you use the simplified scale rulers designed for use with this book. They will enable you to work in scale very easily. The 1/4-in. scale ruler is printed on **Page 229** and should be carefully cut out with scissors.

Referring to **Fig. 5**, you will see how the 1/4-in. ruler provides a means of working accurately in scale.

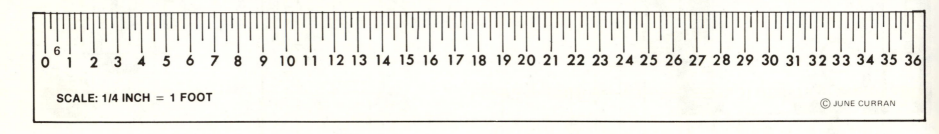

SCALE: 1/4 INCH = 1 FOOT

© JUNE CURRAN

Figure 5.   The simplified 1/4 in.-scale ruler provided with the book.

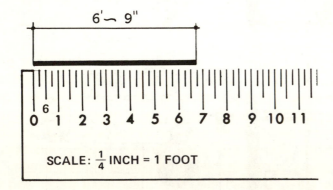

SCALE: $\frac{1}{4}$ INCH = 1 FOOT

NOTE: The zero point on the ruler should be placed at the beginning of the line to be measured. Each large number represents 1 ft. The longer line between numbers represents 6 in. Each short line represents 3 in.

Figure 6.   Measuring a line in 1/4 in.-scale.

20

MEASURING AND DRAWING ON SQUARED DRAWING PAPER

Squared drawing paper (called cross-section or graph paper) is often used by design professionals when drawing plans for a home. Using this type of paper will make drawing easier for you because the scale is already worked out. The squares in **Fig. 7**, as in all the drawings throughout the book, have been reproduced in accurate scale and can be measured with your scale ruler. They are typical of those printed on the type of vellum drafting paper recommended for use with this simplified drawing system. Looking closely at **Fig. 7**, you will see that there are many fine lines and a few heavier ones.

Since 1/4 in. (1/4″) *represents* one ft. (1′) when working in 1/4-in. scale, the space between the heavier lines *represents* four ft. (4′) and the space between each pair of fine lines *represents* six in. (6″).

OBTAINING SQUARED (CROSS-SECTION OR GRAPH) PAPER

Squared drawing paper can be purchased from stationery or artists' supply stores. Squares are printed on both translucent and opaque papers in a variety of sheet sizes and scales. When you purchase a supply for your project, be careful to ask for paper called "vellum," marked off in eight squares to the inch (sometimes written 8 x 8). For this type of work, translucent paper is preferable for two reasons: it is easy to see through when tracing, and it is the correct density for making prints from drawings. Keep in mind that prints (sometimes called blueprints) cannot be made from opaque paper (paper you cannot see through) because light cannot pass through it.

Light blue (drop-out) ink is usually used to print squares on drafting vellum. When a print is made from a drawing prepared on this type paper, the squares drop out (do not appear on the print).

Small sheets of paper, approximately 8 1/2 x 11 in. in size, can be used for many of the projects in this book; however, you will need to purchase larger sheets of paper when you begin drawing a complete house plan. Pads of 18 x 24 in. sheets are available and are adequate for drawing small homes. A variety of larger sheet sizes and roll sizes is also available.

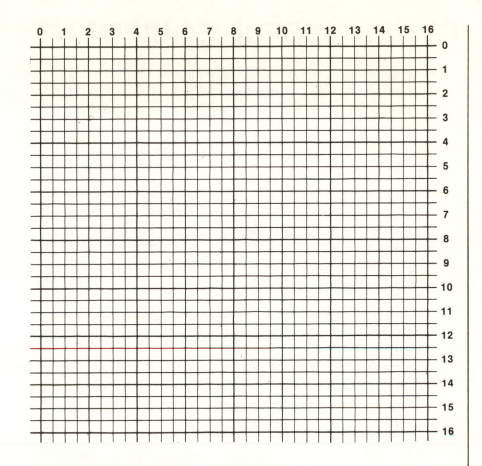

Figure 7.   Measuring on squared drawing paper.

OBTAINING AND USING TRACING PAPER

Tracing or layout paper is inexpensive, thin, translucent paper made strong enough to withstand hard pencil pressure and repeated erasing. It is important for many drawing jobs and can save a great deal of time. By fastening tracing paper over a drawing that has been made on squared drawing paper, you can try ideas without disturbing your original work. There are many grades readily available in stationery and artists' supply stores and it comes in rolls, sheets, and pads of various sizes. Choose the most translucent paper you can find, and use it generously to sketch ideas and to conserve your supply of squared vellum.

OTHER USEFUL EQUIPMENT

The following list of other useful equipment is provided for those who become seriously interested in making detailed and professional looking drawings and wish to acquire a few tools of the trade.

PENCILS

The most readily available pencils are those numbered 2, 2 1/2, or 3. The lead in a No. 2 pencil is medium soft, No 2 1/2 is medium, and No. 3 is medium hard. However, there are pencils and leads made especially for drafting and these are much more satisfactory for drawing home plans. Drawing leads are carefully graded and numbered by degrees of hardness.

6H—5H—3H—2H—H—F—HB—B—2B—3B—4B—5B—6B
HARDEST   INTERMEDIATE   SOFTEST

Wooden pencils (**Item A, Fig. 8**) can be purchased in any of the above degrees of hardness. These pencils are inexpensive and can be sharpened with an ordinary pencil sharpener that grinds off the wood and points the lead simultaneously.

Most drafters use mechanical pencils made especially for drawing leads (**Item B, Fig. 8**). All degrees of leads are interchangeable in these pencils.

My preferences are:

    For layout work, 5H
    For darkening the wall lines, H
    For all other detailing and for dimensioning, 3H
    For lettering, HB or F

If you have a tendency to bear down hard on your pencil as you draw, you may need slightly harder leads.

The B grade leads are too soft for drawing plans. They are most often used for illustrating.

PENCIL SHARPENERS AND LEAD POINTERS

To sharpen wooden pencils, some drafters remove the wood with a pocket knife and rotate the lead on a piece of sandpaper or nail file. Ordinary pencil sharpeners are often satisfactory.

To sharpen the lead in a mechanical pencil, you will need a lead pointer made especially to keep a fine point on the lead (**Item C, Fig. 8**). There are several other kinds of lead pointers available including small pocket pointers. A piece of sandpaper can also be used.

ERASERS

The ruby or pink pearl eraser is the one most suited to the type of vellum drafting paper recommended. It is made of pink rubber with an outer wrapping of paper that peels off, leaving an eraser tip narrow enough for erasing in small areas (**Item D, Fig. 8**). Magic-Rub is a white vinyl eraser that peels off in the same way. This type eraser is very useful for erasing on tracing paper and cleaning smudges from drawings.

COLORED PENCILS

A blue pencil is useful to shade the lines that indicate wall thickness on the floor plan. When a print is made, the blue-pencil shaded lines stand out clearly. Experiment with several different kinds until you find one that goes on the paper smoothly and sharpens easily.

TRIANGLES

Drafters' triangles are made of plastic and come in two shapes. One can be used to draw a 45° angle (**Item G**), the other can be used to draw either a 30° or a 60° angle (**Item F**), depending on how it is placed on the work. Both types are available in several sizes. I prefer a 30° - 60° triangle about 8 in. long for drawing vertical lines on plans for a small home. *Vertical lines* (up and down) are drawn by placing a triangle on the T square, moving it to the desired position and drawing along the long side as shown in **Fig. 8**.

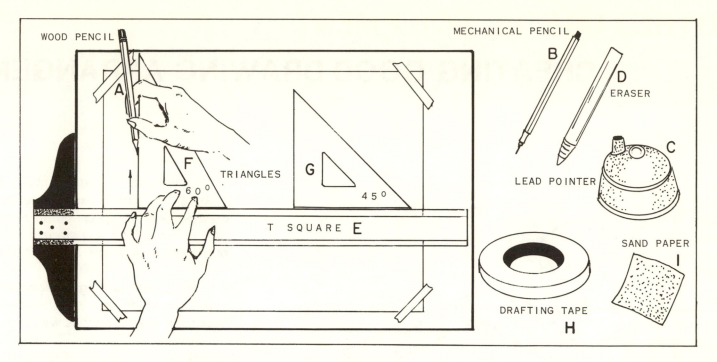

Figure 8.   Examples of other useful equipment.

T SQUARES

The most economical and readily available device for drawing *horizontal lines* (left to right) is the T square (**Item E, Fig. 8**). The T square is used by placing it on a drawing board (the board must be square), pressed tightly against the edge. It is held in place or moved up and down along the board with the left hand, leaving the right hand free for drawing. Reverse this procedure if you are left-handed. When squared drawing paper is fastened to the drawing surface, the lines of the paper must be aligned with the edge of the T square. The T square comes in many lengths. Ideally, the one you obtain should be no longer than the width of your board. It can be a little shorter. The most satisfactory T square has transparent plastic edges along which your pencil glides smoothly. The transparency enables you to see through to your work.

TEMPLATES

When drawing bathroom fixtures, kitchen fixtures and appliances, and door swings on your final plan, you may wish to use a general purpose architects' template instead of tracing from the design guide symbols provided with the book. Architects' templates are usually made of thin, translucent plastic. Openings or cavaties in the plastic are shaped to represent the outline of various symbols. By selecting the required shape on the template and placing it on your plan in the correct position, you can trace the outline, thereby producing a clean and accurate symbol.

CREATING GOOD DRAWING ARRANGEMENTS

Figure 9.   Good drawing arrangements.

Drawing can be done much more easily and accurately if you make a few simple arrangements for comfort and convenience. A **drawing board** propped up on a desk or table is a tremendous help. It can be made from any smooth piece of wood, such as a breadboard or a piece of plywood. It should be thick enough to be rigid.

Art stores carry lightweight, smooth boards of all sizes which are especially made and ideal for this purpose; however, a homemade board will work almost as well.

When this board is placed on a desk or a table with the top edge propped up several inches, the drawing attached is raised to a convenient working angle.

You can prop the top edge of the board up with books, bricks, a piece of 2 x 6 - in. lumber, or anything level and solid.

If your board is not very smooth, fasten a flat, smooth piece of heavy, light-colored cardboard to it for a backing. Plain, smooth, light-colored linoleum also makes an excellent drawing surface.

You can stick cardboard to your board with masking tape, Scotch tape or thumbtacks. Fasten your squared drawing paper to your smooth drawing surface in the same way. Drafting tape, which is quite similar to masking tape, but not so sticky, is excellent for this purpose. It can be obtained at stationery stores.

Good lighting is another important factor in comfortable and accurate drawing. Place the light to your left and slightly behind your shoulder if it is a table or floor lamp. A fluorescent desk lamp can be placed in front of the board so that it shines down on the work.

CHAPTER TWO

STARTING TO WORK IN 1/4-INCH SCALE

PROJECT 2 Thinking In Scale

Objective: *To understand how to measure and draw lines in 1/4-in. scale with the aid of the scale ruler and squared drawing paper.*

Materials Required: *The 1/4-in. scale ruler from the book, squared drawing paper, a pencil, and an eraser*

LEARNING TO THINK AND DRAW IN SCALE

Figure 10. Put your scale ruler to work.

PUT YOUR 1/4-in. SCALE RULER TO WORK:

1. You can put your 1/4-in. scale ruler to work by measuring each of the lines in **Fig. 10**. Write down the length of each line.

2. Check your figures with the answers at the top of the next page.

3. Either by using your scale ruler or by counting the squares on your squared paper, draw the three rectangles shown in **Fig. 11**.

NOTE: Always place the zero point on the ruler at the beginning of the line to be measured.

First rectangle: 4 ft. 6 in. x 3 ft.
Second rectangle: 2 ft. 6 in. x 5 ft.
Third rectangle: 4 ft. x 4 ft.

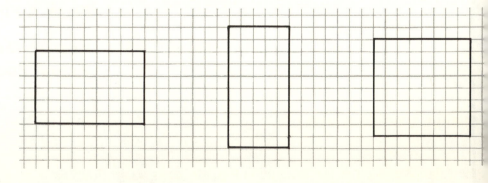

Figure 11. Draw rectangles in scale.

WHAT A FLOOR PLAN IS

When you are drawing plans for a building of any kind, it is necessary to make a drawing which shows the arrangement of rooms, the placement of doors and windows, the location of closets, cabinets, plumbing fixtures, appliances, etc.

A procedure for portraying these details of a building has been devised which, when followed carefully, results in a drawing easily understandable to anyone working with it. This drawing is called a floor plan.

What you see when you look at or draw a floor plan is exactly like what you would see if you had a detailed scale model of a building, and you were looking straight down into it, as in **Fig. 12** on the next page.

SIMPLE EXPERIMENTS:

1. Compare each of the features in **Fig. 12**, used as an example to clarify the meaning of a floor plan, with the corresponding features of the actual floor plan, **Fig. 13**.

NOTE: The dark shaded lines in Fig. 12 indicate walls and conform to the dark, shaded wall lines in the floor plan, Fig. 13. The floor plan is drawn in a scale of 1/4 in. = 1 ft.

2. Observe how each part of the house is indicated on the floor plan drawing. Compare such details as windows, cabinets, and bathroom fixtures.

THE IMPORTANCE OF A FLOOR PLAN

In planning a house, the floor-plan drawing is the one you will be most concerned with. It deals with the most important things, such as the size and shape of the living space in the finished home. This book, therefore, deals first with the floor plan.

Before you can draw a complete floor plan, however, you must learn to think about a home in scale on paper; you must also learn to draw the simple symbols and designations which represent the component parts of a house. Then you will be able to analyze needs for space arrangements in a home and translate them into a scale drawing.

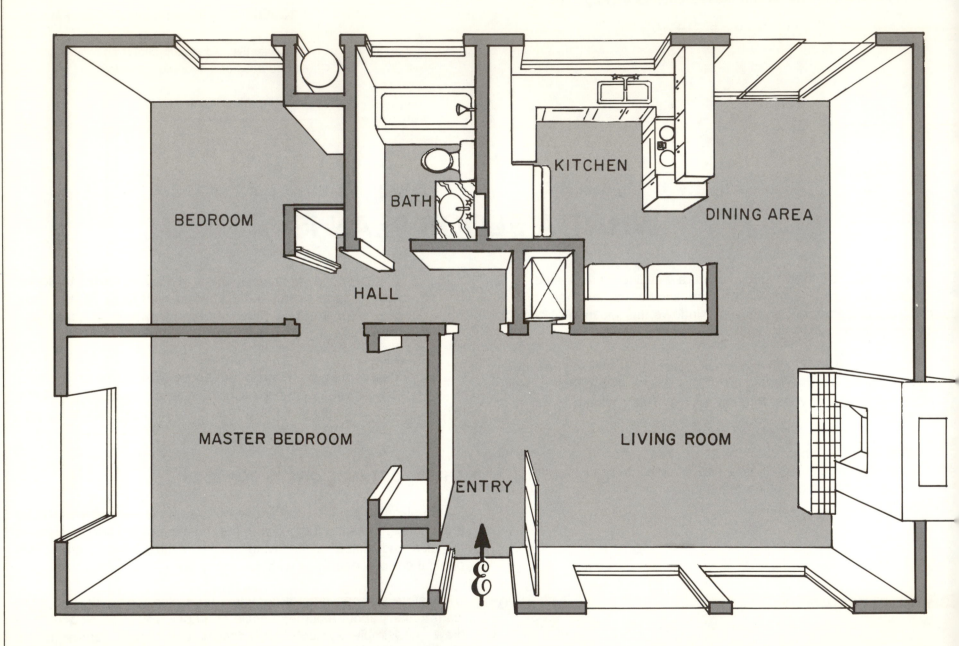

BEDROOM

BATH

KITCHEN

DINING AREA

MASTER BEDROOM

HALL

LIVING ROOM

ENTRY

Figure 12. What a floor plan drawing portrays.

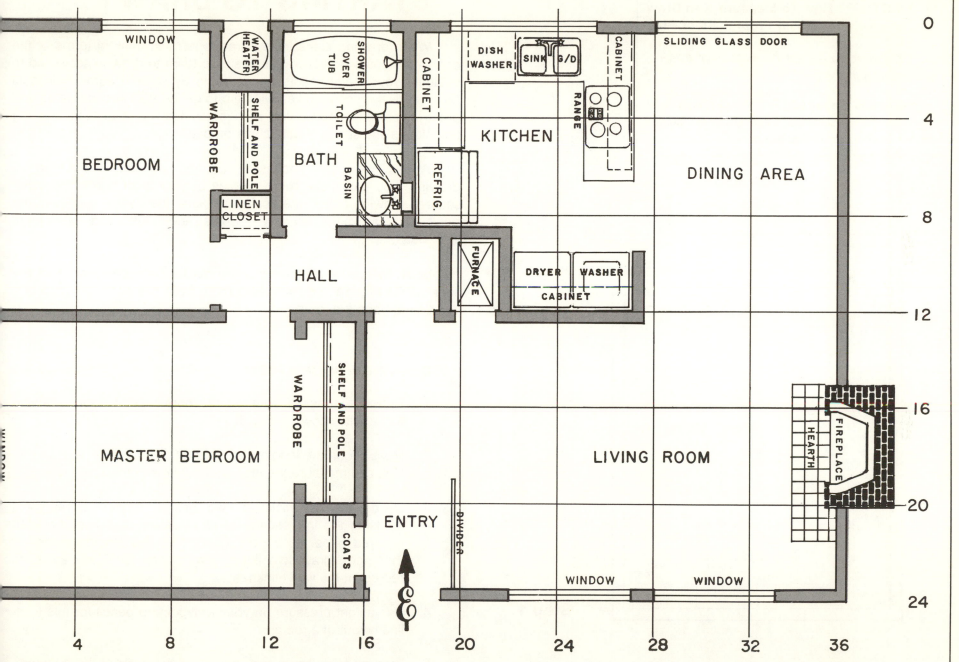

Figure 13.   An actual floor-plan drawing in 1/4-in. scale.

PROJECT 4   How To Measure And Draw
A Room From A Floor Plan

Objective: *To get started measuring, thinking, and drawing in scale.*

Materials Required: *The 1/4-in. scale ruler from the book, squared drawing paper, pencil, eraser, drafting tape, colored pencil*

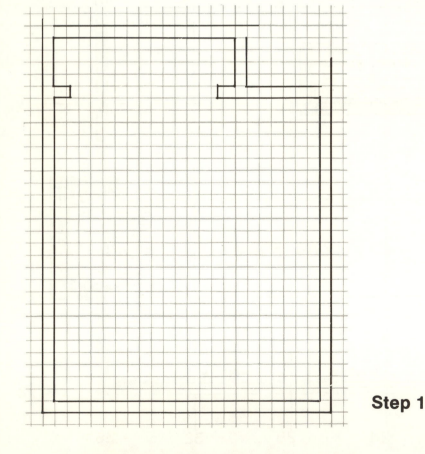

Step 1

3
0

Figure 14.   A light-line layout of the master bedroom taken from the floor plan in Fig. 13.

STARTING TO DRAW

When drawing plans for a home, one must think in terms of the complete house. However, it is easier to learn to draw in scale and to evaluate your requirements if you begin by making some individual room studies. These studies will help to define your requirements and preferences, and enable you to become familiar with plan drawing techniques and space relationships on paper.

Armed with the necessary information and knowledge of drawing, you can make room studies of your own home. By using squared drawing paper, the scale ruler, and the design guides in the book, you can make tentative room arrangements and experiment with ideas.

Begin by making a drawing of the master bedroom taken from the floor plan in **Fig. 13**. You will learn more from this particular project if you do not trace the room.

DRAWING A ROOM STUDY:

1. Fasten a sheet of squared drawing paper to your drawing surface as shown in **Fig. 9**.

2. Measure off the length and width of the room on your paper. You can measure the plan accurately with the scale ruler.

3. Since a wall has thickness, two lines are required to represent it. Using the intersection of two heavier blue lines on your squared paper as a starting point for the outside corner of the room, draw two lines, one square (or 6 in.) apart, to represent the wall thickness.

4. Use a light pressure on your well-pointed pencil for this light-line layout of a room.

5. Proceed to measure and draw in all the walls of the bedroom. Your drawing should look like **Fig. 14**.

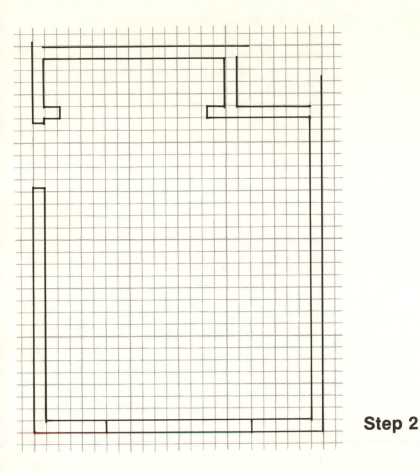

Figure 15.   The same room plan with openings for doors, windows, and closets.

Step 2

6. Measure the room again to determine the location and size of the door, window, and closet openings. Mark their sizes and locations along the wall lines. Erase the wall lines where the door and closet openings are to appear on the drawing. Leave wall lines in where the window is to be. Compare your drawing with **Fig. 15.**

To indicate the window, draw a fine line through the marked-off window-opening space to represent glass. For the closet, draw a fine dashed line to indicate a shelf. Close to it, draw two light lines to indicate a clothes pole, as in **Fig. 16**.

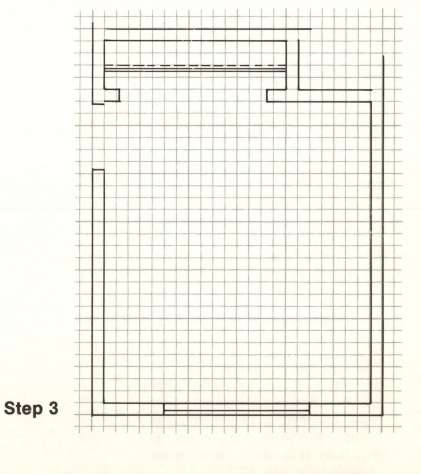

Step 3

Figure 16.   Window and closet details have been added to the plan.

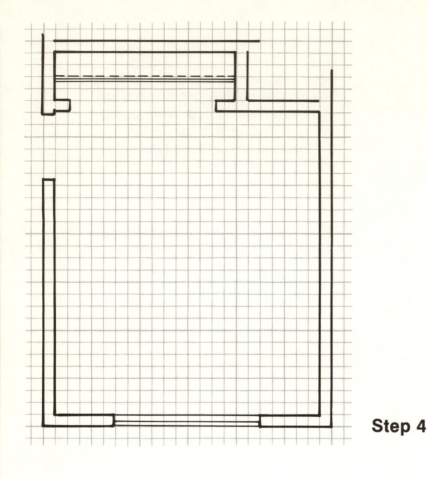

Step 4

Figure 17.   The lines representing walls have been darkened.

9. With a colored pencil (blue, red, or yellow) shade in the lines that indicate wall thickness. Use a light, even pressure on your pencil, making strokes in the same direction as the wall lines. Compare your drawing with **Fig. 18**.

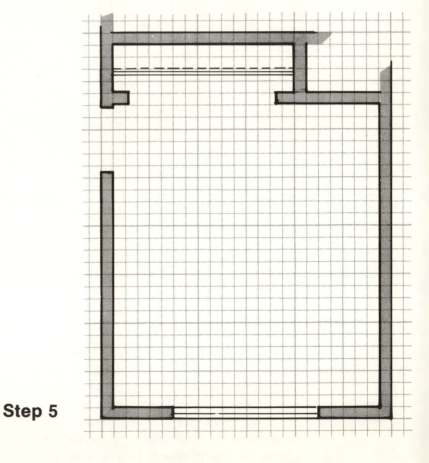

Step 5

Figure 18.   Wall lines have been shaded.

8. The lines that indicate walls are the heaviest lines on the drawing. When you are satisfied that you have them drawn correctly, go over them again, either with a softer grade of lead or with more pressure on your pencil. Compare with **Fig. 17**.

10. Dimensioning your room drawing (writing down the measurements) as you work will save time and give you quick reference. For dimensioning, use a fine, light line made with a well-pointed lead. The lighter lines make dimension lines clearly distinguishable from lines indicating the walls of the structure.

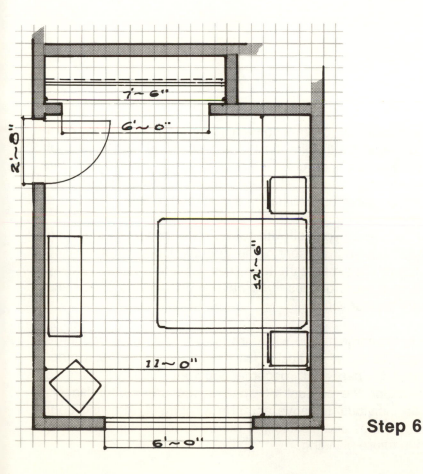

Step 6

Figure 19. Dimensions have been added to the room plan.

PENCIL PROBLEMS

You will notice that your lead wears down quickly. A worn-down lead spoils the appearance of your drawing and a thick line is difficult to measure with a scale ruler. The pencil should be sharpened very frequently while you are doing finishing work. The lead wears more evenly when you rotate the pencil between your thumb and index finger as you draw a line. Also, the correct grades of lead and a good lead sharpener help to make your drawing neater and more precise. See **Page 22**.

NOTE: The dimensioning procedure shown in Fig. 19 will be used with this drawing plans system when drawing individual room studies. Simplified dimensioning procedures for drawing complete floor plans are given in Chapter 9, Project 18.

Objective: *To learn to reduce an actual room and large objects of furniture to a 1/4-in. scale drawing.*

Materials Required: *For measuring a room; a tape measure, yardstick or ruler, scratch pad, and pencil. For drawing; the 1/4-in. scale ruler, design guides, squared drawing paper, pencil, eraser, colored pencil, drafting tape*

JUDGING SPATIAL RELATIONSHIPS

When one attempts to draw something as large as a room on a small piece of paper for the first time, the problem of judging spatial relationships becomes apparent. However, it takes surprisingly little practice with working in scale before one is almost automatically able to judge space on paper as it relates to actual room sizes.

You can familiarize yourself with spatial relationships by selecting one of the rooms in your present home to draw. Choosing the living room or bedroom will simplify the task. You will find it relatively easy to draw your own room because you have lived with the space and are completely familiar with it.

From this experiment, you will learn to reduce a room and large objects of furniture to 1/4-in. scale. Their relationships to each other as they *appear on paper* will become apparent. You will learn to visualize on paper the amount of open space around furnishings needed for an individual to move about in a room. By drawing door and window openings and closets into the plan, you will learn how to handle them in future planning.

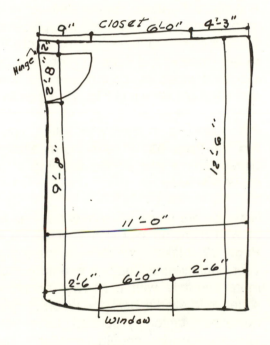

Figure 20.   A rough measurement sketch of an actual room.

MEASURING AN ACTUAL ROOM:

1. On a piece of scratch paper, make a fairly large, rough sketch of the room you have selected to draw. It is necessary to use only a single line, indicating the inside wall, as in **Fig. 20**.

2. Mark along the wall lines on your sketch the approximate location of each door, window, closet, and any other projections or recessed areas in the room.

3. Using a yardstick or a pocket tape measure placed on the floor, start measuring in a corner. Measure from the corner to the first door, window, or other break in the wall. Write the measurement on your sketch. Then write down the size of the door, window, etc., and continue measuring around the room, writing the figures on your sketch as you go. See **Fig. 20**.

    NOTE: Do not include moldings, trims, baseboards, etc. Actual wall-to-wall measurements and actual sizes of the openings are needed.

4. After measuring around the room, measure its length and width. Total your first figures and compare them with your length and width measurements. This procedure will ensure accuracy.

5. Check to see that you have included such things as projecting registers or any permanent fixtures. Note whether the doors open into the room or out from it. Also note whether they are hinged on the left or on the right, as in **Fig. 20**.

CONVERTING YOUR MEASUREMENT SKETCH TO A 1/4-INCH SCALE DRAWING

1. Fasten a sheet of squared drawing paper to your drawing surface as in **Fig. 9**. If the room is oblong, the widest side of the paper should be placed on the board horizontally (left to right). Make sure that you start your drawing far enough to the left and from the top of the paper so that the entire room will fit on the sheet with space enough left for dimension lines.

   NOTE: To help you understand easily the first drawing you made (taken from Fig. 13), the illustration was planned so that the wall lines came out exactly on the squares. However, when you are drawing an actual room in an existing house, your measurements will probably not come out exactly on the squares. If you will get used to using your scale ruler, you will find that the inch marks indicated on it will make accurate representation of feet and inches very easy.

2. By using your scale ruler from the kit or by counting the squares on your paper, convert the actual room measurements to 1/4-in. scale measurements and lay out the room on your paper. Begin by drawing a light, fine line to represent the inside of each of the four walls. Moving back one square (or 6 in.) from the first lines, draw another line all the way around the outside of the first to allow for the thickness of the walls. Since the measurements you made were for the inside of the room, the overall measurements of the drawing will be about 12 in. larger, allowing for the thickness of the two walls.

3. Add the projections, offsets, or closets from your sketch to your drawing in accurate scale. You have now reached the stage of plan development shown in **Fig. 14, Page 30**.

4. Referring to your sketch, determine the location of windows and doors. By using your scale ruler or counting the squares, mark along each wall line the placement of the openings. Erase the lines to leave spaces where the door openings are to be. Draw in fine lines to represent glass where you have indicated windows. Your drawing is now in the stage of plan development shown in **Fig. 16**, **Page 31**.

5. Put in dimension lines with a fine, light pencil as shown in **Fig. 19**, **Page 33**. Write in the measurements lightly. Making dimensions a part of the drawing at this stage gives you quick reference.

6. Now you are ready to go over the wall lines with a softer lead or with more pressure on your pencil as shown in **Fig. 17, Page 32**. Make your dimensions more distinct by erasing your original notations one at a time and then putting them in more carefully with a heavier pressure on your pencil. A softer lead works best for lettering. Most drafters use light guidelines, uniformly spaced, for all lettering and numbers. These guidelines should be slightly less than one square apart.

7. Shade the wall thickness with a colored pencil as indicated in **Fig. 18**, **Page 32**.

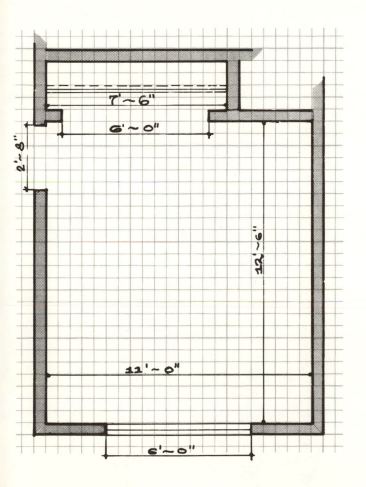

Figure 21.   An example of a completed room drawing.

8. Now you are ready to add furniture to the drawing. You will find, on the design guides, many different sizes, shapes, and types of furniture. Measure each piece in your room and make a note of its width, depth, and height on your rough sketch. Choose the item of furniture from the design symbols that is closest in size to your piece. Trace it on the plan in the correct position. See **Fig. 21**. Keep in mind that the figures on the design guides indicate inches.

9. Study your finished drawing and compare it with your room to become familiar with the way *actual* sizes and shapes appear on paper in 1/4-in. scale.

PENCIL PROBLEMS

If the lead and the colored pencil smear, making an unattractive drawing, check on the following things:

1. Are you completing your drawing with light pencil lines before going over the walls with heavier lines?

2. Is the lead you are using for your layout work hard? Is it sharply pointed?

3. Does your eraser do a clean and thorough job?

4. Have you used the colored pencil lightly?

5. Are your hands smearing areas you have already drawn as you work on other, clean areas? If so, try covering finished areas with a piece of tracing paper to keep them clean while you work on the rest of the drawing.

CHAPTER THREE

HOW TO DRAW IN 1/8- AND 1/16-INCH SCALE

PROJECT 6   Learning to think in 1/8-in. and 1/16-in. scale.

Objective: *To become familiar with smaller scales sometimes used in the preparation of plot plans and house plans.*

Materials Required: *The 1/8-in. and the 1/16-in. scale ruler cut from Page 229, squared drawing paper, pencil and eraser*

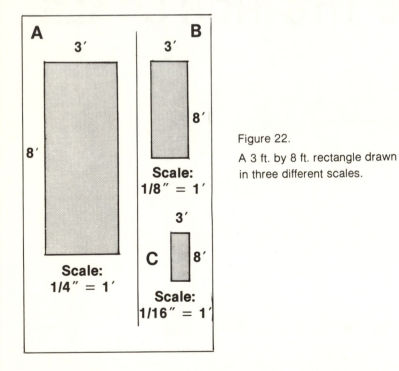

Figure 22.

A 3 ft. by 8 ft. rectangle drawn in three different scales.

4
0

NOTE: The sides of the 1/4-in. scale rectangle (A) are exactly twice as long as the sides of the 1/8-in. rectangle (B); similarly the sides of (B) are twice as long as the sides of (C).

DRAWING IN 1/8-IN. AND 1/16-IN. SCALE

Although most floor-plan drawings are done in 1/4-in. scale, other scales are sometimes used for special purposes. For example, in instances where the subject to be drawn is too large to fit on paper of a convenient size, smaller scales are an advantage. Consequently, plot plan drawings (drawings of a plot of ground or a lot) are often drawn in a scale in which 1/16 in. is equal to 1 ft.

Rulers in 1/8-in. and 1/16-in. scale have been provided with the book to make it easy for you to measure and draw in scales smaller than 1/4 in. Carefully cut them out with scissors from **Page 229** .

Since you have already learned to think and draw in 1/4-in. scale, you have acquired basic knowledge that will enable you to understand other scales.

COMPARING SCALES:

1. Refer to **Fig. 22 A, B, and C**. You can see how the 3 x 8-ft. rectangle drawn in a scale of 1/4 in. = 1 ft. (A) compares in appearance with a rectangle of the same dimensions drawn in a scale of 1/8 in. = 1 ft. (B) and in 1/16 in. = 1 ft. (C).

2. Try measuring and drawing rectangles in 1/8-in. and 1/16-in. scale with your scale rulers as shown in **Fig. 23**.

NOTE: When working in 1/8-in. scale, each square on the drawing paper is equal to one foot. When working in 1/16-in. scale, each square is equal to 2 ft.

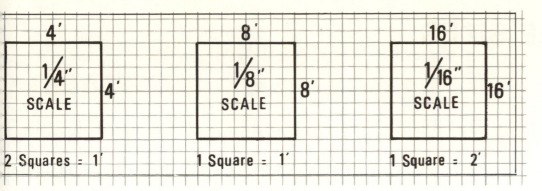

re 23. Comparative scale measurements on squared paper.

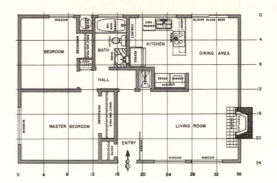

Figure 24. 1/16-in. scale drawing.

FLOOR PLANS IN SMALLER SIZES:

1. In order to visualize scales smaller than 1/4 in., compare **Figs. 24** and **25** with **Fig. 13**, on **Page 29**. These three illustrations are of the same plan. **Fig. 13** was drawn in 1/4-in. scale. **Fig. 24** has been reduced to 1/16-in. scale and **Fig. 25** has been reduced to 1/8-in. scale.

2. **Figs. 26-28** are drawings of scale rulers in 1/4- 1/8- and 1/16-in. scales. These same rulers are printed on cardboard, on **Page 229**. If you have not already done so, cut them out with scissors.

3. Compare the scales indicated on each of the three rulers.

Figure 25. 1/8-in. scale drawing.

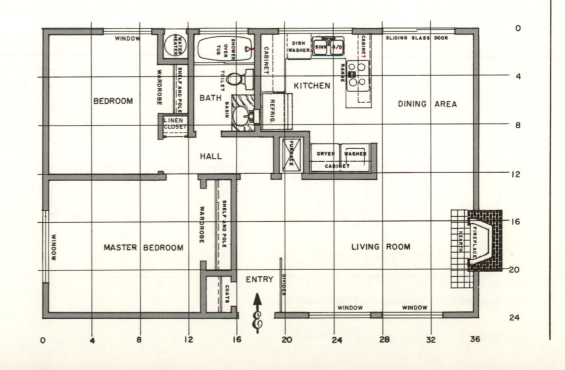

SCALE RULERS IN THREE SIZES

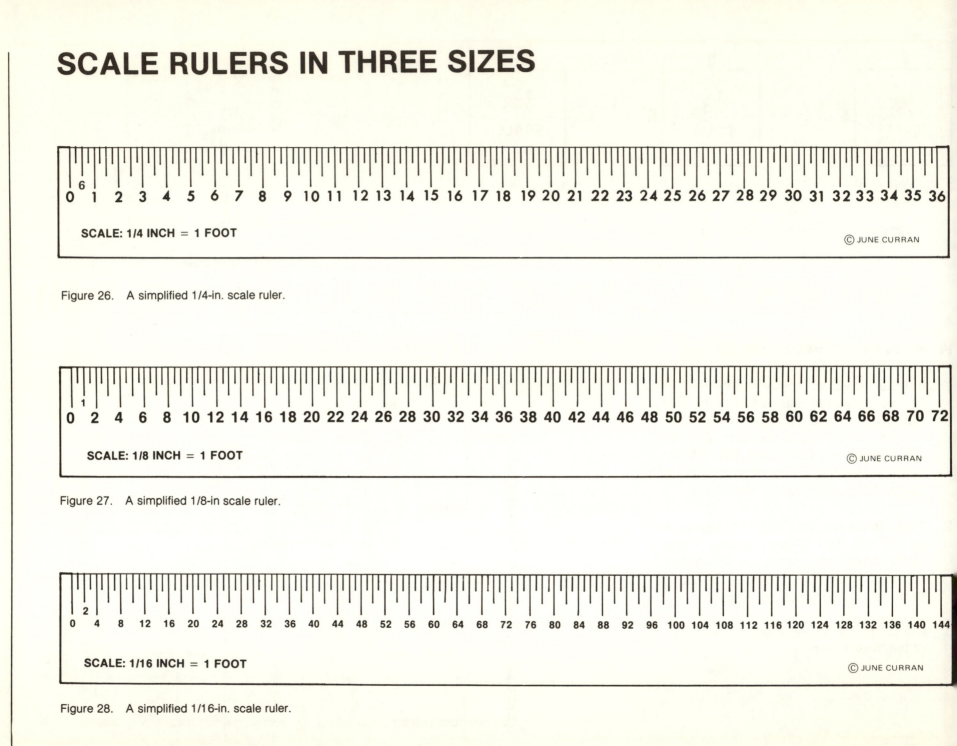

SCALE: 1/4 INCH = 1 FOOT

© JUNE CURRAN

Figure 26.   A simplified 1/4-in. scale ruler.

SCALE: 1/8 INCH = 1 FOOT

© JUNE CURRAN

Figure 27.   A simplified 1/8-in scale ruler.

SCALE: 1/16 INCH = 1 FOOT

© JUNE CURRAN

Figure 28.   A simplified 1/16-in. scale ruler.

CHAPTER FOUR

DRAWING A PLAN OF THE BUILDING SITE FOR NEW HOMES...ADDITIONS... REMODELING

43

PROJECT 7   **Drawing A Plot Plan**

Objective: *To learn to draw a plan of a lot in scale, showing existing features and space available for construction.*

Materials Required: *The 1/16-in. scale ruler cut from Page 229, squared drawing paper, a map or sketch showing the measurements and all other available information about the property, pencil, eraser, drafting tape*

OVER-ALL PLANNING OF HOUSE AND LOT

Drawing a floor plan which seems to have suitable space arrangements for individual requirements is just one phase of home planning. A truly well-planned home is only achieved when over-all planning of house and lot result in the maximum use of every foot of lot space. The use of outdoor living space should be given equal consideration with that of indoor living space.

WHAT IS A PLOT PLAN?

A plan of a lot is referred to as a plot plan. A plot plan is a drawing of a plot of ground or lot. Visualize a plot plan the same way as you would visualize a floor plan. Imagine that you are directly above the lot, looking down on it. Any buildings, trees, or other three-dimensional objects would *appear* to be flat. The land would also *appear* to be flat, even if it were sloping or contoured.

PLANNING A NEW HOME ON A PLOT PLAN

A careful study of the use of the entire lot will result in an attractive and convenient arrangement for the house, driveway, car shelter, and service and garden areas.

When you plan the best use of lot space before starting to draw floor plans for the project, good interior space arrangements will become evident. In turn, plans for interior space arrangements will influence decisions about exterior shape and style.

PLANNING A REMODELING PROJECT ON A PLOT PLAN

A plot plan of the lot, showing the existing house, garage or carport, driveway, and all the other features of the lot, will help you to make plans for a *remodeled* home that relates well to the site.

PLANNING AN ADDITION ON A PLOT PLAN

A plot plan of the lot showing the existing house and any other structures on the lot is essential when planning an *addition*. The plan will reveal available space for the new *addition* and help you to make the best possible use of lot space. The plot-plan drawing will also be required when you make application for building permits for the new *addition*.

SUBDIVISION MAPS

Fig. 29 is an example of a plot plan for a level lot, rectangular in shape, measuring 70 ft. in width and 100 ft. in depth. This drawing shows lot boundary lines only.

The information needed to draw this plot plan was taken from a portion of a subdivision map. A copy of the portion of the subdivision map on which the buyer's lot is located is usually included with the buyer's papers at the time the lot or home is purchased. These maps are quite small and contain limited information; however, you can obtain exact boundary locations and dimensions of the lot from them. The buyer is entitled to receive a map of the property, so be sure to obtain one.

TO DRAW A PLOT PLAN:

1. Using the 1/16-in. scale ruler provided with the book, draw a plot plan of the lot on squared drawing paper, using a line composed of one long dash and two short ones, as shown.

2. If you are *remodeling* or *adding* to a home, you can measure the lot or take the information from the papers you received at the time of purchase.

3. If you have no lot, but wish to draw this project, choose an average city lot size of 50 x 100 ft. or 60 x 100 ft. to experiment with.

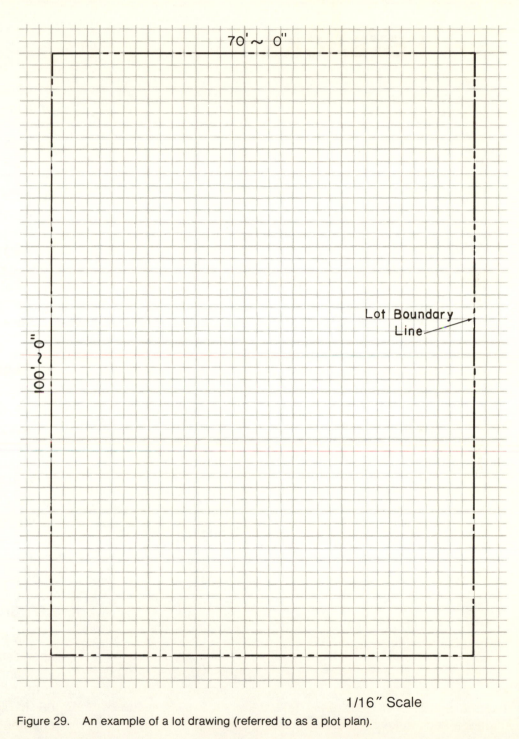

1/16″ Scale

Figure 29.   An example of a lot drawing (referred to as a plot plan).

SETBACKS

Setbacks are requirements regarding the placement of a house on a lot. City or county planning departments in each area require that houses be set back from the lot boundary lines a certain distance. Typically, a setback of 15 to 20 ft. is required from the street front boundary line to the front of the house; 5 ft. is required from each side boundary line of the lot to each side of the house. A minimum of 15 ft. is required from the back boundary line to the back of the house. Refer to **Fig. 30**.

NOTE: Setback requirements vary in different communities and if you are building a new house or making an addition to a home it is important to check with your city or county planning department when you are ready to draw a plot plan of the lot.

INDICATING SETBACK REQUIREMENTS ON A PLOT PLAN:

1. When you have drawn your plot plan boundary lines and verified local setback requirements, indicate setbacks as shown in **Fig. 30**. Copy the short dashes used for this purpose.

2. As an example, take 20 ft. as the front setback, 5 ft. on each side as the side setbacks, and 15 ft. as the rear setback.

3. When a plot plan has been drawn with the setbacks lightly indicated, it is easy to visualize the available space for the construction of a house and other facilities or an addition on the lot.

LOT SPACE YOU CAN BUILD ON

In **Fig. 30**, you see that the maximum width available on the lot, after deducting setbacks, is 60 ft. Since the lot is 100 ft. deep and the front and back setbacks combined total 35 ft., the remaining lot depth is 65 ft. There are any number of possibilities for the use of this 60 x 65 ft. space; some of these are described further along in this chapter.

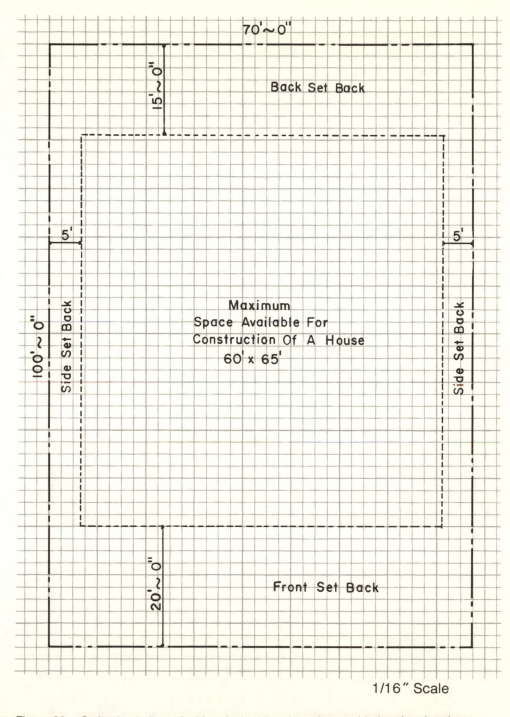

NOTE: When the car shelter is located on the back of the lot, codes sometimes permit placement as close as 5 ft. from the back lot boundary. See Fig. 38, Page 56.

1/16″ Scale

4
7

Figure 30.   Setbacks, indicated with a dashed line, have been added to the plot plan.

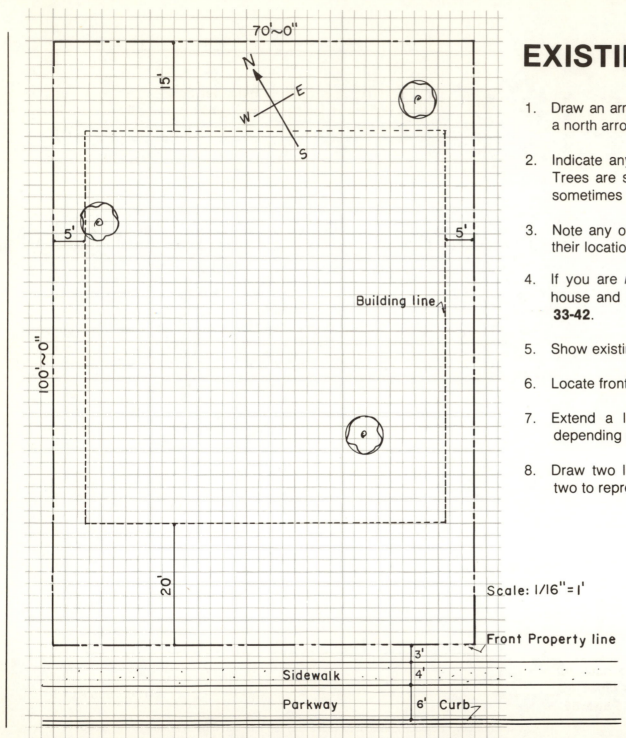

70'~0"

15'

N
E
W
S

5'   5'

Building line

100'~0"

20'

Scale: 1/16" = 1'

Front Property line

3'
Sidewalk   4'
Parkway   6' Curb

EXISTING FEATURES

1. Draw an arrow to indicate north on the plot plan. You will find a north arrow on your subdivision map. See **Fig. 31**.

2. Indicate any trees growing on the lot which are to remain. Trees are sometimes drawn with a symbol, as shown, and sometimes with a plus mark (+).

3. Note any other existing features or buildings on the lot and their locations. See **Fig. 32**.

4. If you are *remodeling* or making an *addition*, measure the house and garage and draw them on the lot. Refer to **Fig. 33-42**.

5. Show existing sidewalks and driveways as in **Fig. 33**.

6. Locate front sidewalks and curbs.

7. Extend a line from the front property line about 13 ft., depending on your local requirements.

8. Draw two lines across the page to represent the curb and two to represent the sidewalk, as shown in **Fig. 31**.

Figure 31. Preparing a plot plan.

5. Place the scale indication - 1/16″ = 1′ - at the bottom of the plot plan.

6. Cover your plot-plan drawing with tracing paper. Placement of the new work, such as house, garage, driveway, and walks can now be worked out on the tracing paper, leaving the plot plan clean. It is best to complete the final plot-plan drawing after the working drawings are completed. See **Fig. 118** on **Page 126**.

NOTE: The property between the front property line and the curb belongs to the city. Sidewalks and parkways are usually installed in accordance with city specifications.

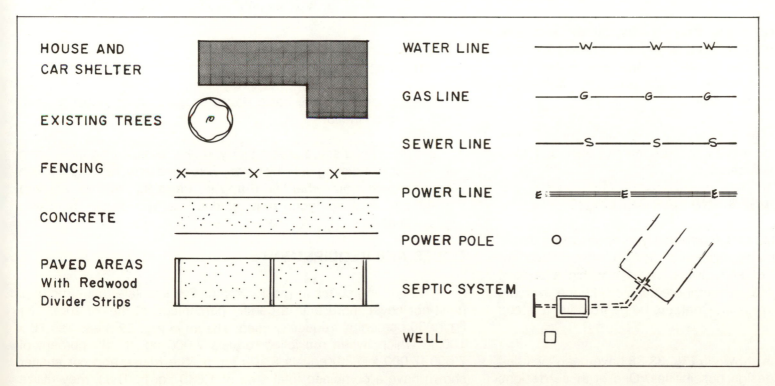

HOUSE AND CAR SHELTER		WATER LINE	——W——W——W——
EXISTING TREES		GAS LINE	——G——G——G——
FENCING	×——×——×	SEWER LINE	——S——S——S——
CONCRETE		POWER LINE	E====E====E==
PAVED AREAS With Redwood Divider Strips		POWER POLE	O
		SEPTIC SYSTEM	
		WELL	□

Figure 32.   These symbols are used in plot-plan drawing.

49

BASIC HOUSE SHAPES

Since the house must fit the lot, it is logical to begin the preliminary planning on your plot plan. If you are making plans to *remodel* or *add on* to an existing house, the plot plan, showing the size and shape of the existing house, garage, driveway, walks, and porches or patios will be extremely helpful.

When drawing plans for a new home or an addition, very important preliminary planning will be done on the plot plan, and it will serve as a guide during construction.

BASIC SHAPES FOR HOUSES AND CAR SHELTERS

A house can be any size and shape that you choose to make it, as long as it fits within the limitations of the lot area, allows for convenient arrangement of other facilities, and fits within a budget. Lot shapes vary greatly. Some are simple rectangles like the example in **Fig. 33**. Others are very irregular. Contours range from flat to steep hillsides.

The basic house shapes shown in **Fig. 33-38** have been included to introduce you to a few design possibilities. One of these designs may serve to guide you in starting your plans.

Each of the basic shapes shown on the next few pages has unique possibilities for arrangement of interior space and interesting use of lot space.

STUDYING BASIC HOUSE SHAPES:

1. As you study the basic house shapes, try to visualize each one on the lot.

2. When you see a shape that you like, sketch it on the tracing paper covering your plot plan. This need only be a light, rough sketch, somewhat like **Fig. 100, Page 95** . In this way you can evaluate your requirements as you study the basic shapes.

CODES AND REQUIREMENTS

The building codes in most communities stipulate that structures must not cover more than a certain percentage of the lot area. The figure 30 percent is frequently used. The lot in **Fig. 33** measures 70 x 100 ft. which, when multiplied, equals 7,000 sq. ft.; 30 percent of 7,000 (7,000 x 0.30) equals 2,100 sq. ft. The house and car shelter shown have a combined total area of 1,840 sq. ft. Thus, they utilize less than 30 percent of the lot area.

KEY

1 Terrace
2 Screened service area
3 Pool, 18-ft. diameter
4 Trash cans

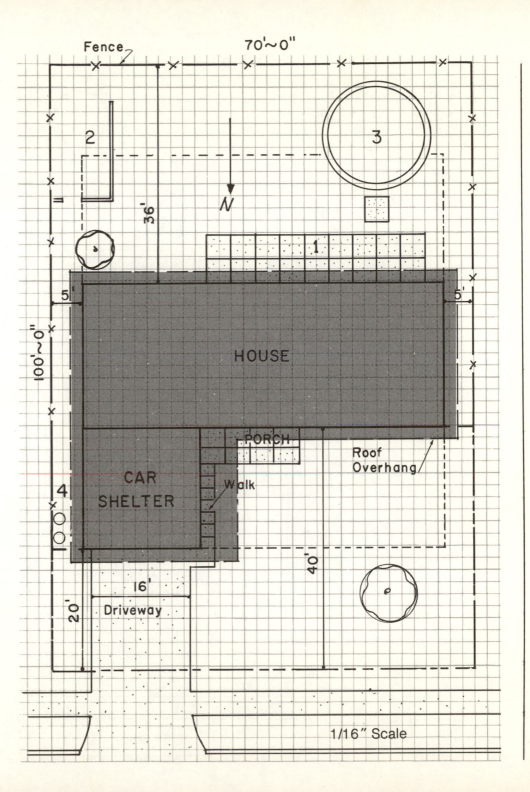

Figure 33. An example of an **L**-shaped house on a 70 ft. x 100 ft. lot.

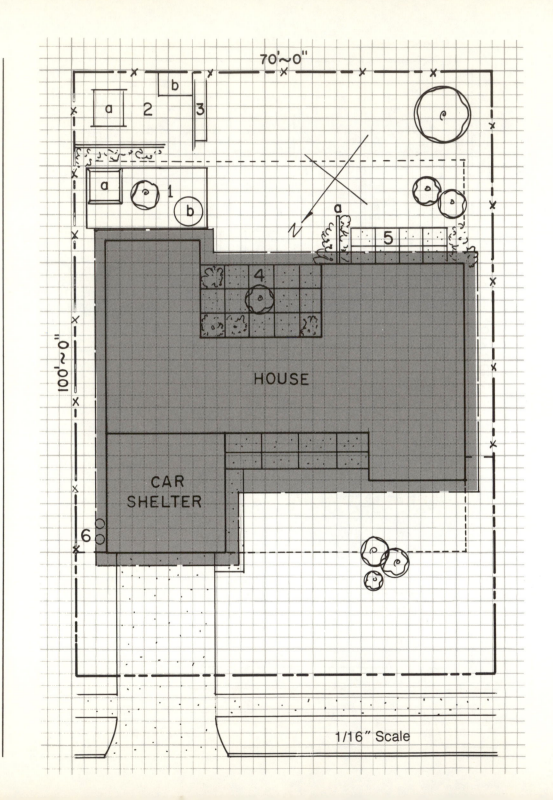

70'~0"

b

a 2 3

a 1

b

a

5

4

HOUSE

CAR SHELTER

6

100'~0"

1/16" Scale

KEY

1 Children's play area
   a. Sand box, 4 ft. x 4 ft.
   b. Wading pool, 4 ft.
2 Service area
   a. Clothes line, 5 ft. x 6 ft.
   b. Tool storage, 4 ft. x 6 ft.
3 Potting bench
4 Dining terrace
5 Master bedroom
   terrace, 6 ft. x 16 ft.
   a. Privacy screen
6 Trash cans

An advantage of an H-shaped house is the sheltered courts or terraces created by the wings of the building. The minimum practical distance between wings, (across courts) is 10 ft. The total area of this house and car shelter is 1,904 sq. ft.; the total area of the lot is 7,000 sq. ft.; 30 percent of 7,000 sq. ft. is 2,100 sq. ft.

Figure 34.   An example of an **H**-shaped house on a 70 ft. x 100 ft. lot.

KEY

1 Pool, 16 ft. x 34 ft.
2 Screened service area
3 Terrace
4 Terrace
5 Storage
   a. Tools
   b. Trash cans
6 Screened entrance court

The T shape could be positioned in several ways on the lot. It might also be a good solution for an irregularly shaped lot. This plan is oriented in such a way as to permit maximum sun in the pool area. Total area of house and car shelter: 2,072 sq. ft.; total area of lot: 9,020 sq. ft.; 30 percent of 9,020 sq. ft. = 2,706 sq. ft.

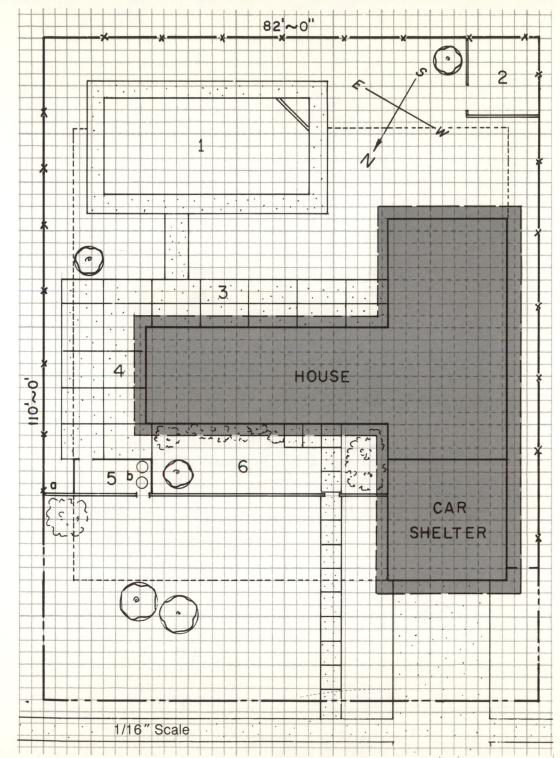

1/16" Scale

Figure 35. An example of a **T**-shaped house on an 82 x 110 ft. lot.

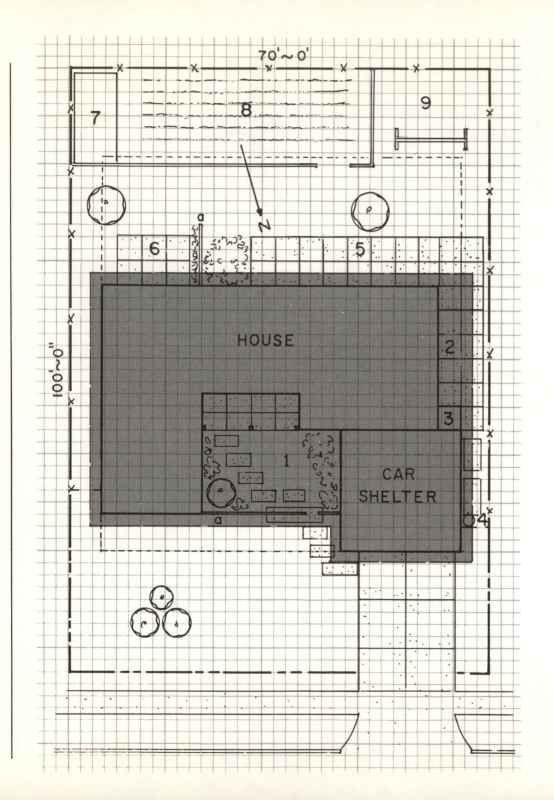

70'~0'

100'~0"

7

8

9

6

5

HOUSE

2

3

1

a

CAR SHELTER

4

KEY

1 Atrium
   a. Privacy screen
2 Dining terrace
3 Storage
4 Trash cans
5 Sitting terrace
6 Master bedroom terrace
   a. Privacy screen
7 Greenhouse
8 Vegetable garden
9 Children's gym set,
   12 ft. x 8 ft.

The atrium, or court, could also be facing the back garden or either side of the lot. The garden and terrace areas are oriented on the lot in such a way as to obtain morning sun and late afternoon shade in the summertime. Total area of house and car shelter: 1,872 sq. ft.; total area of lot: 7,000 sq. ft.; 30 percent of 7,000 sq. ft. = 2,100 sq. ft.

Figure 36.   An example of a **U**-shaped house on a 70 ft. x 100 ft. lot.

KEY

1 Dining and sitting terrace
2 Firewood storage, 4 ft. x 8 ft.
3 Clothes line, 8 ft. x 20 ft.
4 Tool storage
5 Family orchard
6 Trash cans

The rectangular shape in this design is economical to build and leaves more lot space for outdoor living than is available with the preceeding plans. Total area of house and car shelter: 2,088 sq. ft.; total area of lot: 7,000 sq. ft.; 30 percent of 7,000 sq. ft. = 2,100 sq. ft.

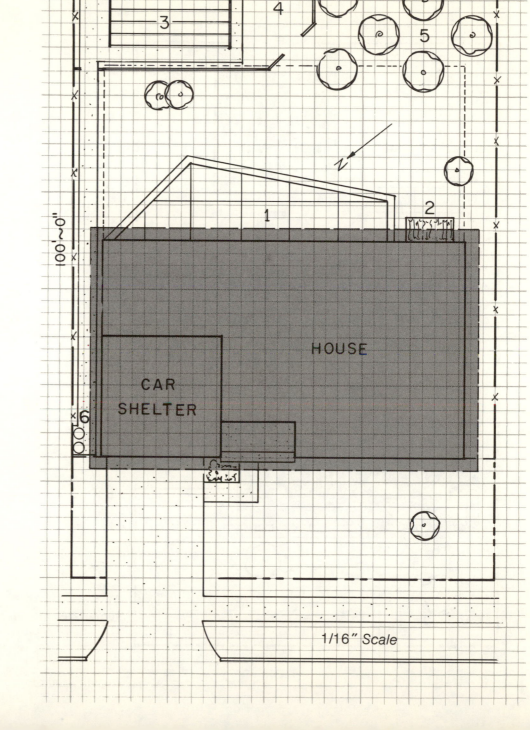

1/16" Scale

Figure 37.   An example of a **RECTANGULAR** house on a 70 ft. x 100 ft. lot.

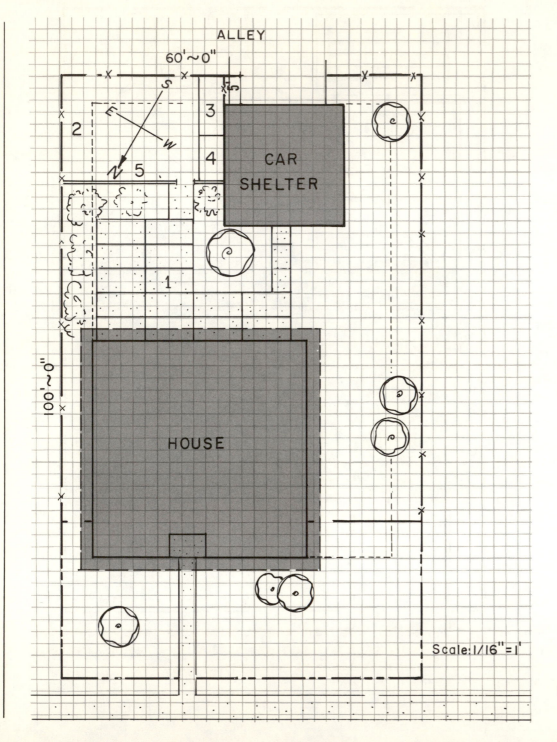

ALLEY

60'~0"

CAR SHELTER

HOUSE

Scale: 1/16"=1'

KEY

1 Dining and sitting terrace
2 Service area
3 Potting bench
4 Storage for tools and garden furniture
5 Screen

The plot plan in **Fig. 38** shows a 60-ft.-wide lot, situated on an alley. A garage or carport can be placed as close as 5 ft. to the rear property line under certain circumstances. If you are planning to place the car shelter at the rear of the lot, but must have a driveway in the side yard, you will need a minimum of 8 ft. between any obstruction (house, steps, etc.) and the property line. The square shape of this house makes it very economical to construct. Total area of house and car shelter: 1,696 sq. ft.; total area of lot: 6,000 sq. ft.; 30 percent of 6,000 sq. ft. = 1,800 sq. ft.

Figure 38. An example of a **SQUARE** house on a narrower, 60 ft. x 100 ft. lot located on an alley.

MAKING THE BEST USE OF THE LOT SPACE

One plan for a house and car shelter can be placed on the plot-plan drawing in a number of different ways. **Project 12** on **Page 97** and **Project 13** on **Page 98** give instructions for starting to draw a floor plan of your own design.

You may feel restricted in drawing your plan because of lot limitations. However, a little experimentation will show that there are a number of ways in which the house can be placed on the lot. After you draw the house on the lot in several ways, the most desirable one will become evident. **Figures 39-42** show examples of the same house and car shelter placed on a lot in four different ways.

When planning the house to fit the lot, study all of the things which would have an effect on its livability. Such things as the proximity of the closest neighbors, the way their windows face, and the location of their driveways can be extremely important.

By planning carefully, you can make the maximum use of the lot space, you can create space for a private patio, a children's play yard viewable from the kitchen or family room, if needed, and many other features.

MAKING A STUDY:

1. Become familiar with the arrangement examples shown on the next few pages. They will give you some idea of the many different effects which can be achieved by carefully planning the house to fit the lot.

2. Experiment with the arrangements on tracing paper fastened over your plot plan.

3. Determine the most convenient place on the lot for a driveway and car shelter in relationship to a kitchen and service area and to the neighbors' houses.

4. Be aware of unattractive features which should be screened out and of attractive features which can be incorporated in the planning.

NOTE: You can create privacy and beauty in the surroundings which will have a very lasting and very real effect on ones enjoyment of the home.

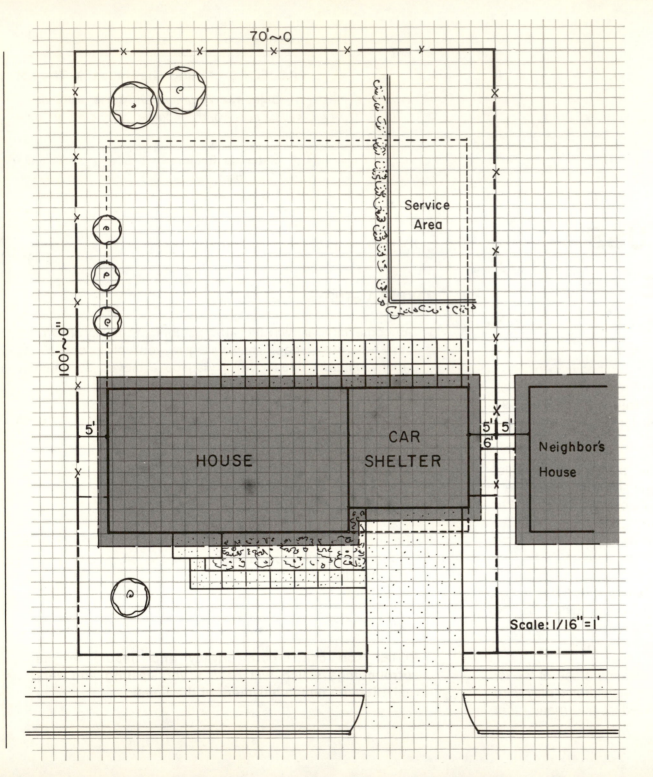

70'~0

100'~0"

Service
Area

HOUSE

CAR
SHELTER

5'

5' 5'
6'

Neighbor's
House

Scale: 1/16"=1'

When the house you are designing and the neighbor's house have roof overhangs, the minimum distance between the outer edges of each should be 6 ft.

Figure 39. Example arrangement, No. 1.

It is usually permissible to build to the back of the lot, as long as the setback requirement is observed. This arrangement is particularly suitable on a narrow lot.

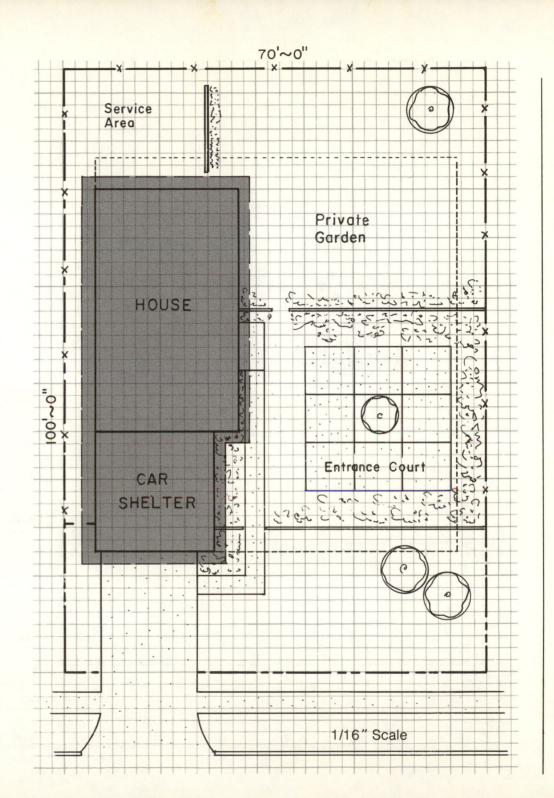

Figure 40.   Example arrangement, No. 2.

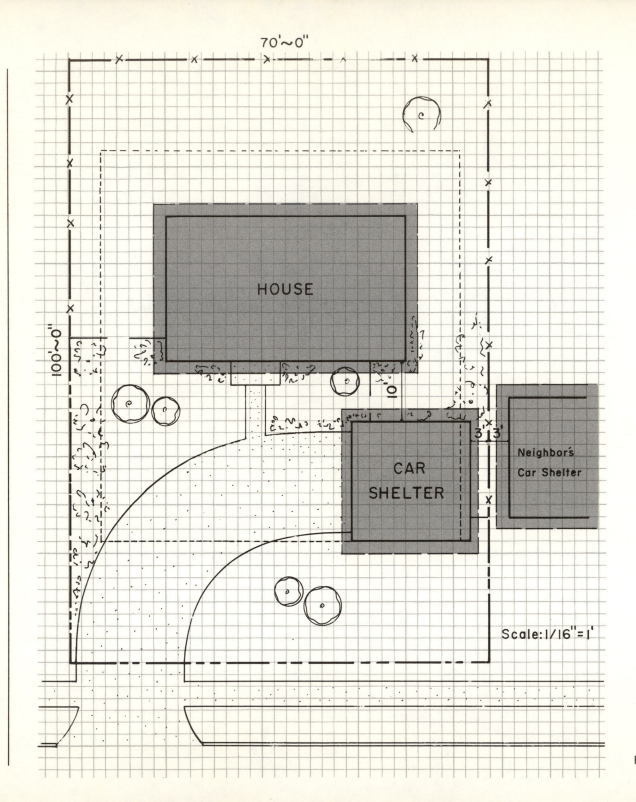

70'~0"

100'~0"

HOUSE

10'

CAR SHELTER

3' 3'

Neighbor's Car Shelter

Scale:1/16"=1'

The minimum required space between the house and the car shelter, in most cases, is 10 ft. However, when there are no windows in either facing wall, this requirement may be reduced to 5 ft. The regulation is for fire protection and does not apply when the house and car shelter are connected with a roof, usually called a breezeway. In cases where a car shelter is adjacent to the neighbor's car shelter and separate from the house, some codes permit placing it within 3 ft. of the property line. See **Fig. 41**.

If the neighbor's house is adjacent to one's garage or carport and is at least 7 ft. from the property line, one can place the garage within 3 ft. of the property line in most cases. This plan (**Fig. 42**) offers maximum privacy from the street. The screen between the house and the car shelter could be a high wall. The arrangement creates a sheltered, roofed atrium.

Figure 41. Example arrangement, No. 3.

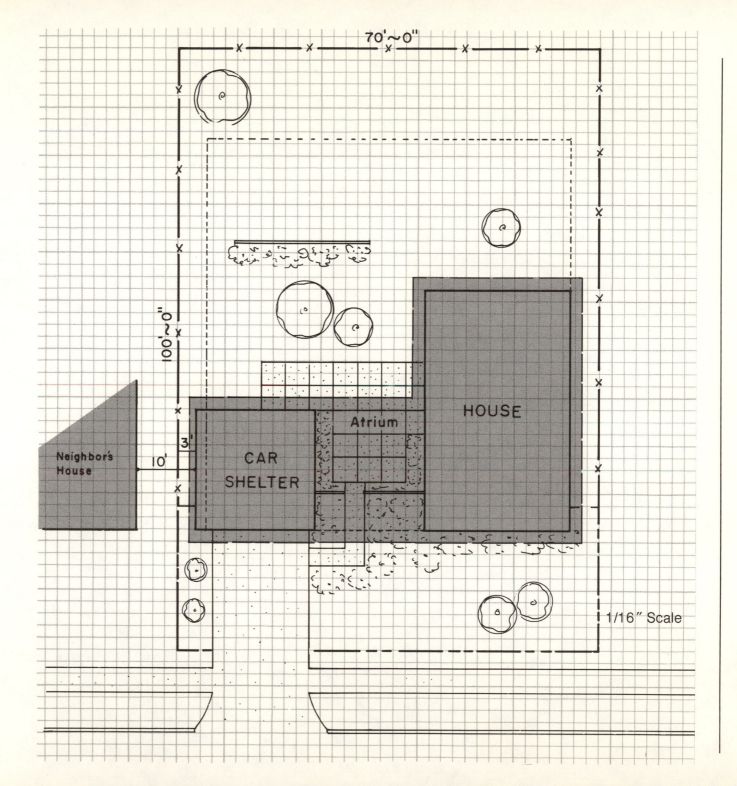

70'~0"

100'~0"

HOUSE

Atrium

CAR
SHELTER

Neighbor's
House

3'

10'

1/16" Scale

6
1

Figure 42.   Example arrangement, No. 4.

CHAPTER FIVE

SYMBOLS, SIZES, AND DESCRIPTIONS FOR DRAWING AND READING PLANS

PROJECT 10   **Learning To Recognize And Draw Symbols And Designations**

WHAT ARE SYMBOLS AND DESIGNATIONS

This chapter contains information about each of the component parts of a house. Sizes and space requirements are given as well as possible selections and the symbols and designations used to represent each part. Necessary space allowances have also been given. The descriptions of available materials and fixtures will help with selections.

Symbols and designations, as used on floor plan drawings, are marks that represent each of the component parts of a house. Since all of the marks are symbolic of the items they represent, it is easy to use them. These symbols and designations have become standardized and are recognized and understood by most everyone involved in the business of construction and design.

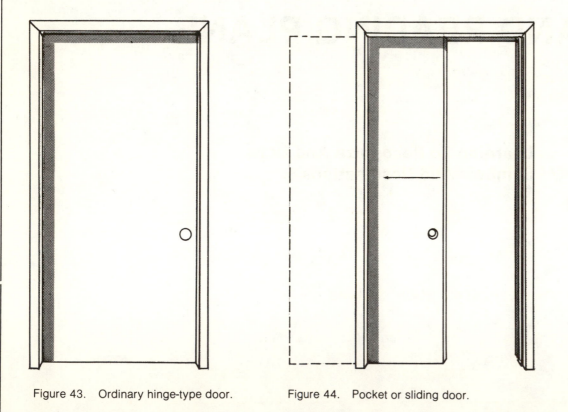

Figure 43.   Ordinary hinge-type door.   Figure 44.   Pocket or sliding door.

SELECTING AND DRAWING INTERIOR AND EXTERIOR DOORS

HINGE DOORS

The most commonly used doors in a residence are the ordinary hinge-type shown in **Fig. 43**. They may be hinged to swing either from the right or from the left side of the opening. They can open either into the room or out, away from it. **Figure 45** shows the correct designation for drawing door swings for hinged doors.

POCKET DOORS

The pocket door is one which slides back into a pocket in the wall. It can be planned to slide to either the right or the left, depending on the space available in the wall. **Figure 44** shows a pocket or sliding-type door. The pocket door is especially convenient in places where the swing of the door interferes with furniture or traffic paths. **Figure 45** shows the correct designation for drawing pocket-type doors.

NOTE: In indicating door sizes, the width is always given first, as 3 ft.-0 in. x 6 ft.-8 in., usually stated and written as 3^0 x 6^8. Garage door information is given in Project 16, Figures 113 and 114.

DOOR SIZES

Manufacturers have standardized door sizes. If any of the standard sizes shown in **Fig. 45** are selected, one would find them available wherever building materials are purchased. These sizes apply to both hinge-type and pocket-type doors. The smallest door opening one can walk through comfortably is 2^0. 2^0 doors are sometimes used in bathrooms. Other doors in a house should be 2^2, 2^6, or 2^8. Consider the size of furnishings to be moved in and out of rooms when choosing door sizes. Doors leading out of the house or to an attached garage are usually 3^0.

TO DESIGNATE DOOR SWINGS ON THE PLAN:

1. Door-swing designations are on the design guide sheets and may be on your general-purpose template. See **Fig. 45**. The straight line indicates the door. The arc indicates the swing of the door.

2. Study your furniture plan and traffic paths when deciding whether to use right or left door swings or pocket doors. See **Fig. 107**.

3. In **Figure 99** doors have been added to the floor plan.

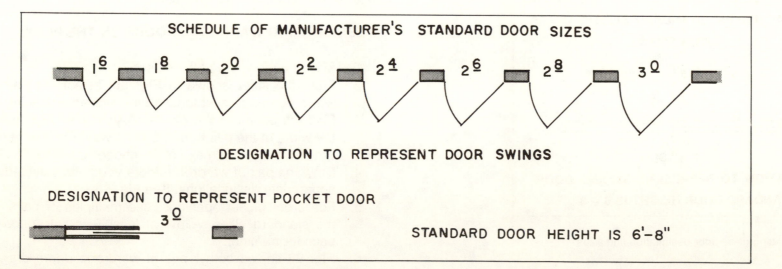

SCHEDULE OF MANUFACTURER'S STANDARD DOOR SIZES

1^6 1^8 2^0 2^2 2^4 2^6 2^8 3^0

DESIGNATION TO REPRESENT DOOR SWINGS

DESIGNATION TO REPRESENT POCKET DOOR

3^0

STANDARD DOOR HEIGHT IS 6'-8"

Figure 45.   Designations to represent doors.

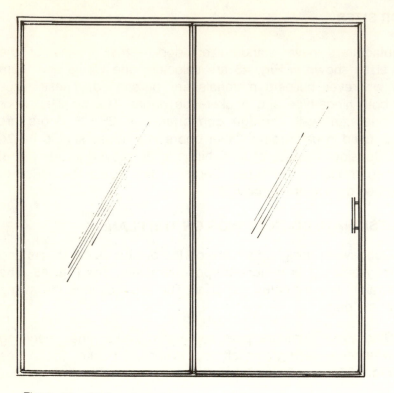

Figure 46. Sliding glass door.

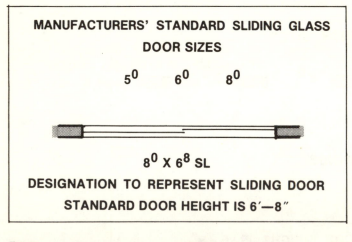

MANUFACTURERS' STANDARD SLIDING GLASS DOOR SIZES

5^0 6^0 8^0

8^0 X 6^8 SL

DESIGNATION TO REPRESENT SLIDING DOOR
STANDARD DOOR HEIGHT IS 6'—8"

Figure 47. Sliding glass door designation and sizes.

SLIDING GLASS DOORS

Sliding glass doors are used in instances where a large glass area, as well as access to a patio, is desirable. They are sometimes referred to as patio doors. These doors are made with two glass panels mounted in a frame. One panel remains in a fixed position. The other panel slides back. They can be ordered with either the right or the left panel sliding. Most are interchangeable. For cold climates they are available with double glazing. A sliding glass door is shown in **Fig. 46**.

DESIGNATING SLIDING GLASS DOORS ON THE PLAN:

1. The symbol for drawing sliding glass doors is shown in **Fig. 47** and on the floor plan **Fig. 99** on **Page 92**.

WARDROBE DOORS

Bifold and sliding doors are two commonly used types of wardrobe doors. The bifold is made from pairs of narrow folding doors as shown in **Fig. 48**. Pairs of sliding doors, sometimes called bypass doors, are depicted in **Fig. 49**.

DESIGNATING WARDROBE DOORS ON THE PLAN:

1. Measure the width of the closet.
2. From the sizes shown in **Fig. 50**, select the pair of doors which comes closest to fitting the available opening space.
3. Find the center of the closet on your plan and mark off half the width of the pair of doors each way from the center point. Erase wall lines to make a closet-door opening.
4. Draw the pair of wardrobe doors you have selected, using the appropriate designations. See **Fig. 50**.
5. For larger closet openings, use multiples of pairs of any of the standard sizes. Allow at least 6 in. of space between pairs for framing.
6. **Fig. 99** shows both types of wardrobe doors drawn on the floor plan.

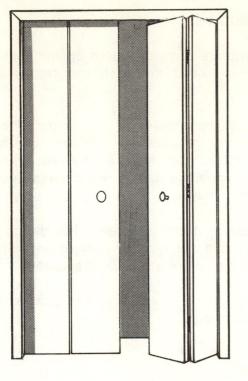

Figure 48.   Bifold wardrobe door.

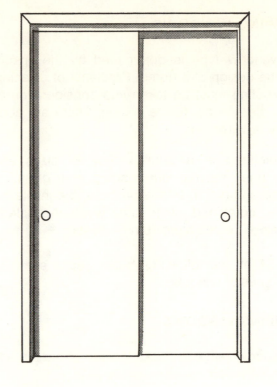

Figure 49.

Sliding wardrobe door.

NOTE: When indicating wardrobe door sizes, the width is always given first, as 6 ft-0 in. x 6 ft-8 in.

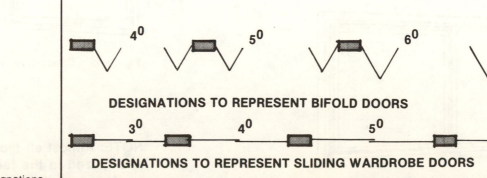

SCHEDULE OF MANUFACTURER'S STANDARD WARDROBE DOOR SIZES

2^0 2^6 3^0

STANDARD WARDROBE DOOR HEIGHTS ARE 6′—8″ and 8′—0″.

4^0 5^0 6^0

DESIGNATIONS TO REPRESENT BIFOLD DOORS

3^0 4^0 5^0 6^0

DESIGNATIONS TO REPRESENT SLIDING WARDROBE DOORS

Figure 50.   Wardrobe door sizes and designations.

67

SELECTING AND DRAWING WINDOWS

The suitability of a window type is determined by the special requirements inherent in the design of a home. Problems of cleaning, ventilation, and weatherproofing must be taken into consideration as well as the adaptability of the window to the design. There are good window types to suit every requirement.

Windows are manufactured in a great variety of sizes and materials. Window sash (the material surrounding the glass) is manufactured of both wood and metal. In one process, the insulating properties of wood are combined with the weather-resistant, maintenance-free properties of treated aluminum or plastic.

Figures 51 through 54 on the following pages depict some of the most commonly used types of windows.

HORIZONTALLY SLIDING WINDOWS

Horizontally sliding windows slide in tracks located at the top and bottom of the frame.

They are divided into two or more panels. One half is usually fixed, and the other half slides, allowing 50 percent ventilation. The screen fits on the outside.

An advantage of these windows is that there are no projections when the window is open. Also, large sizes are more practical in this type. They are available in wood, metal, or wood covered with either aluminum or plastic.

Figure 51.   Horizontally sliding window.

DOUBLE-HUNG WINDOWS

Double-hung windows are commonly used in new construction. They are also extensively used to match existing windows in remodeling.

In this type of window, both halves of the window slide up and down and are held in the desired position by balanced counterweights attached to each side of the sash. Newer double-hung windows have a spring or spiral mechanism which operates the same way as the counter weight. They also have neatly fitted screens.

This window is useful in extreme climates. The design assures minimum air infiltration when the window is weather-stripped. For more weather protection, a double-glazed type is available.

Double-hung windows come in wood, metal, or wood covered with either aluminum or plastic.

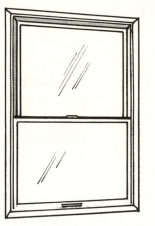

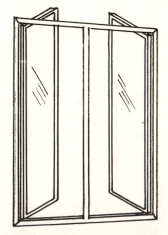

Figure 53.   Casement window.

Figure 52.   Double-hung window.

NOTE: Almost all types of windows are fully assembled and glazed in the factory; they are delivered to the job ready to install.

CASEMENT WINDOWS

Casement windows have panels hinged at the side of the sash. The panels usually swing outward for weathertightness. The screens and storm sash must be on the inside. They are constructed of both wood and metal. Double-glazed types are available for extreme weather conditions.

The chief advantage of this window is that it can be opened entirely, permitting 100 percent ventilation. This may be the correct window to use in cases where maximum ventilation is important.

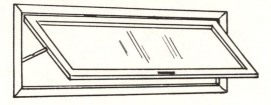

Figure 54.   Awning window.

AWNING WINDOWS

Awning-type windows are made to swing outward at the bottom with hinges at the top. They are constructed of both wood and metal in a variety of sizes and weights and can be obtained double-glazed and weather-stripped. Awning windows can be used singularly or in groups.

These windows are especially adaptable for basements and above or below fixed picture windows for additional ventilation. They are inexpensive and utilitarian and give 100 percent ventilation.

NOTE: The description of a window 6 ft.-0 in. wide by 3 ft.-0 in. high would read or be written 6 0 x 3 0. Manufacturers shorten the description by leaving out the foot and inch marks. The 0 indicates no inches.

TO DESIGNATE WINDOWS ON THE PLAN:

1. In the drawing plans system, all window types are drawn in the same way on the floor plan.
2. **Figure 55** shows the designation to use in drawing windows. When your planning has progressed to the point that you can decide on the sizes of windows, you can write in the size as shown.

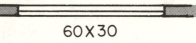

60 X 30

Figure 55.   Window designation.

DESIGNING WINDOW SIZES:

1. When planning window widths on paper, draw them in even measurements of 12 in., as 2 ft., 3 ft., 4 ft., etc. These window sizes are more likely to be available in the type of window eventually chosen for the home. Since there are so many kinds and styles on the market, it would be best to consult manufacturers' literature for exact sizes in the final stages of planning.
2. The height of the window off the floor is also a consideration. This height will not affect your drawing while you are working on floor plans but it is helpful to have some idea of height in mind when drawing windows into the plan. Since the tops of the windows will be the same height as the tops of the doors, this height is used to determine how far from the floor the windows will be.
3. As an example, assume that you choose to use a standard window, 3 ft. high. If it is installed at the usual height of 6 ft. 8 in., there would be 3 ft.-8 in. from the bottom of the window to the floor.
4. In deciding on the height of a window, it is helpful to have your furniture plan to refer to. See **Fig. 109**, **Page 109**.

NOTE: When indicating window sizes, the width is always given first, as 8 ft.-0 in. x 3 ft.-0 in.

69

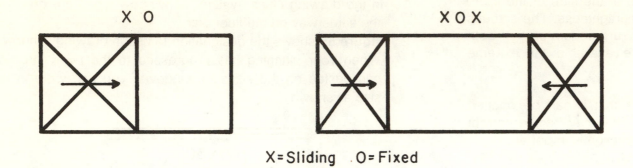

X = Sliding   O = Fixed

Figure 56.   Manufacturers' designations for fixed and movable panels.

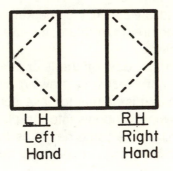

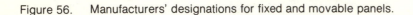

L H   R H
Left   Right
Hand   Hand

Figure 57.   Manufacturers' designation for right- or left-hand opening.

DESIGNATING FIXED AND MOVABLE PANELS ON ELEVATION VIEWS:

1. When planning horizontal sliding windows and sliding glass doors, you can specify which panels are to slide open and which are to remain fixed (not movable).
2. **Figure 56** shows the manufacturers' method of designating fixed and sliding panels.
3. Casement windows can be obtained with panels which open on either the right or left side, or on both sides.
4. **Figure 57** shows the manufacturers' method of indicating which panels open. The unmarked panel is fixed.
5. For designating windows on elevation views of drawings, see **Fig. 145**.

SELECTING AND DRAWING FOR THE BATHROOM

The average bathroom is quite small, yet it contains several large plumbing fixtures, some cabinetry, and (sometimes) other equipment. Making a plan that will accommodate all this in an efficient and convenient arrangement takes careful planning and drawing.

Now, more than ever before, bathroom fixtures are available in a beautiful selection of colors, materials, and styles. There are so many new and interesting possibilities that bathroom planning is a stimulating challenge. The sizes and shapes of plumbing fixtures given on these pages are typical of the average sizes available.

SHOWERS

The symbol for a shower is shown in **Fig. 58** and on the design guides. The small circle in the center of the cross mark indicates the shower drain. The cross mark indicates the slope of the bottom of the shower to the drain. In some showers the drain is located at one end rather than in the center as shown in **Fig. 58a.** This affects the plumbing and should be verified when you select the shower.

BATHTUBS

The symbol for a bathtub is shown in **Fig. 59** and on the design guide. All bathtubs except special-order types are 60 in. long. The standard bathtub is 30 in. wide. The newer models, including those of fiberglass and acrylic, are 32 to 34 in. wide.

TO DESIGNATE SHOWERS AND BATHTUBS ON THE PLAN:

1. If you are using a template, select the fixture of your choice.
2. Place the template on your drawing so that the tracing opening is in the desired position.
3. If there are shaded lines around the shower and bathtub openings on your template, they indicate walls and should be placed exactly over the walls on your drawing.
4. If you are not using a template, trace from the design guides on **Page 221.**

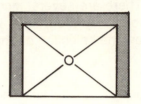

Figure 58.   Symbol for shower with drain located in the center.

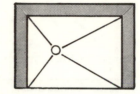

Figure 58a.   Symbol for shower with drain located at one end.

SHOWER OVER

Figure 59.   Symbol for bathtub with shower over.

DESIGNATING A SHOWER OVER THE TUB:

1. If you plan to have a shower over the tub, draw the symbol as shown in **Fig. 59** and write "Shower Over."
2. Shower heads are installed at the same end of the tub as faucets and can be any height you specify.

TO DESIGNATE ENCLOSURES ON THE PLAN:

There are several kinds of enclosures for showers and bathtubs. The following information will help with selections and show you how to draw the selection on the plan.

Figure 60.   Symbol for curtain rod.

Figure 61.   Symbol for hinge-type shower door.

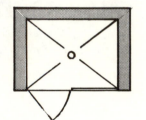

Figure 62.   Symbol for sliding-type shower door.

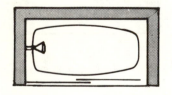

Figure 63.   Symbol for folding-type shower door.

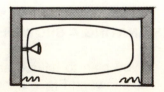

If the plan is to use a **shower curtain** as an enclosure for the shower or bathtub, the only designation needed is:

1.   Two lines indicating the rod on which the curtain hangs.
2.   **Figure 60** shows how this is drawn on the plan.

Shower door enclosures are frequently made of glass or plastic. Half of the enclosure is fixed securely in place. The other half is hinged and swings open. For this type of enclosure:

1.   A straight line (as for glass) designates the fixed half of the opening.
2.   A door swing is drawn on the other half.
3.   The door swing can swing from either the right or the left.
4.   Either side can be fixed in place.
5.   It can also swing into the shower if space is a problem.
6.   See **Fig. 61**.

Sliding door enclosures are made for both bathtubs and showers. In this kind of enclosure, two metal-framed panels of glass or plastic fit into tracks located at the top and bottom of the bathtub or shower. Each panel slides back its full width, permitting an opening one-half the width of the tub or shower. If glass doors are selected, be sure that the glass is tempered (heat strengthened).

1.   The correct designation for a sliding door enclosure is shown in **Fig. 62**.

Another kind of enclosure used on both bathtubs and showers is the **vinyl folding door**. These doors fold back (like an accordian pleat) and have hardware which fits into channels at the top and bottom of the shower or bathtub. The vinyl enclosure glides along the channel when the panel is opened or closed. About 80 percent opening is permitted with this type of door and all danger of shattering glass is eliminated.

1.   The designation for folding vinyl doors is shown in **Fig. 63**.

COUNTER TOPS, BASINS, AND VANITIES

One may choose a counter top, basin, and vanity from a wide selection of beautiful designs. The choice of basin is dependent in most cases on the choice of counter top. There are basins made for installation with each of the various kinds of tops.

When a **plastic laminate** (known under several brand names such as Formica) is used, a hole the size of the basin is cut out of the vanity top. The basin, usually round or oval, fits into the hole and is trimmed with a metal rim.

Basins are made specially for use with **tile**. They fit into a cutout in the supporting base. The tile is usually installed with special tile trim that fits over the edge of the basin, though there are other methods of installation suited to different basin designs.

For **marble-like acrylics**, the installation procedure and choice of basin is the same for plastic laminate.

A **self-rimmed basin** is a design that can be used with any of the above counter tops. The basin is designed in such a way as to eliminate the need for a metal rim around the basin.

One-piece units are another kind of acrylic unit, the basin and vanity top are molded in one piece, eliminating the joint between basin and top.

Basins are also designed for use without vanity cabinetry. Most models of this type are called **wall-hung basins**. There are also models with a single leg in the center which conceals the pipes. Both types are drawn in the same way.

Vanity cabinet selection is not dependent on the type of counter top selected. Vanity cabinets are made to fit any of the different standard sized tops. Manufactured drawer and cabinet units come in many lengths and can be combined to fit almost any space requirement.

TO DESIGNATE COUNTER TOPS ON THE PLAN:

1. It is only necessary to draw the simple symbols shown in **Fig. 64** to indicate any of the preceding material selections.

DESIGNATING VANITIES AND BASINS ON THE PLAN:

The depth (front to back) measurements of the average vanity cabinet is 22 in.

1. Draw a line indicating the correct depth on your plan.
2. Choose whatever length the space permits unless the plan is to use a pre-manufactured unit of a specific size.
3. If you are using a template, select the basin and place it in the desired position within the vanity lines and draw around the opening.
4. If you are not using a template, trace from the design guides on **Page 221**.
5. The basin does not have to be centered in the counter top. Place it where you want it.
6. **Figure 64** depicts a vanity, counter top and basin.
7. **Figure 65** depicts a wall-hung basin.

Figure 64.   Symbol for a vanity cabinet, counter top, and basin.

Figure 65.   Symbol for a wall-hung basin.

Figure 66.   Symbol for a built-in medicine cabinet.

Figure 67.   Standard toilet.

Figure 68.   Deluxe toilet.

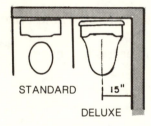

STANDARD   15"

DELUXE

Figure 69.   Symbol for standard and deluxe toilets.

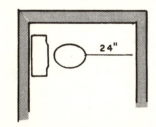

24"

Figure 70.   Space requirements around toilets.

NOTE: Building codes differ slightly in some communities and space requirements may vary.

MEDICINE CABINET DESCRIPTION AND SIZES

Medicine cabinets are designed to fit between the spaces in the framing. The cabinet part which fits into the wall is approximately 14 in. wide and 24 in. high. The mirror is slightly larger. There is also a taller model which measures approximately 30 in. high. Another special model is double width, approximately 28 in. wide. Installing the double-width type involves a little more carpentry.

DESIGNATING A MEDICINE CABINET ON THE PLAN:

1. **Figure 66** shows how to draw a medicine cabinet on the plan.

TOILETS

Toilets are available in many designs and colors. Basically, however, there are only two possible shapes to choose from in drawing your plan. In **Fig. 69** they are designated "Deluxe and Standard". Each represents a different style, but they both require the same space on your drawing.

Standard indicates the design in which the tank is located behind the toilet and is higher than the toilet. See **Fig. 67**.

Deluxe indicates the design in which the tank is low and the entire unit is made in one piece. See **Fig. 68**.

DESIGNATING TOILETS ON THE PLAN:

1. To draw a toilet on your plan, refer to **Fig. 69**. This drawing shows the toilet located close against the wall behind it. If you are using a template, draw around the opening; otherwise, trace from the design guides, **Page 221**.
2. The minimum required distance from the center of the toilet to the nearest wall or cabinet is 15 in. The lines on each side of the toilet in **Fig. 69** show the space requirements.
3. Another important measurement is the space in front of the toilet. You must have a minimum of 2 ft. clearance between the toilet and a wall or cabinet. See **Fig. 70**.

SELECTING AND DRAWING FOR THE KITCHEN

Kitchens have been transformed by beautiful new and improved designs in appliances, cabinetry, and other equipment. However, basic sizes, shapes, and installation procedures of most of the components which make up a kitchen remain very nearly unchanged.

The sizes and shapes of kitchen equipment on the design guides are approximately the same as those of average equipment available. Though one product varies slightly from another, sizes are so nearly standard that the design guides are adequate for most kitchen planning. When the final selection of appliances and cabinetry is made, the manufacturer will furnish literature giving exact sizes and installation instructions. Any small changes in size can be made on the plan at that time.

TO PLAN THE KITCHEN:

1. Begin your kitchen plan by deciding on the most convenient location for the sink, range, and refrigerator.
2. Plan the cabinet layout around these units.
3. Draw lines on the kitchen plan 24 in. inside the walls to show where the outer edge of the cabinets will be.
4. **Figure 71** shows the first stage of a kitchen layout. It is taken from the kitchen in the plan on **Fig. 13**, **Page 29**.

SINK SIZES

There are three sink sizes given on the design guides as shown in **Fig. 72**. The first, measuring 32 x 21 in., is an average-size double sink. The second, measuring 42 x 21 in., is a large double sink. The third, measuring 30 x 21 in., is an average-size single sink.

TO DESIGNATE A SINK ON THE PLAN:

1. If you are using a template, select the sink and decide where to place it.
2. Draw around the opening.
3. Otherwise, trace from the design guides on **Page 221** as in **Fig. 73**.

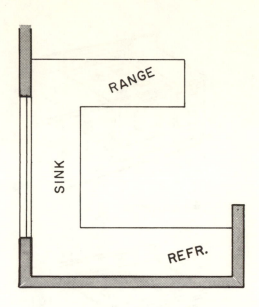

Figure 71. Kitchen layout showing tentative arrangement of sink, range, refrigerator, and cabinets (base cabinets).

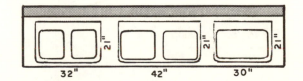

Figure 72. Average sink sizes.

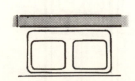

Figure 73. Symbol for double sink.

Figure 74. One-piece range.

Figure 75. Cooking top.

Figure 76. Wall oven.

RANGES

Ranges are available in many styles and a variety of combinations of range tops and ovens. From the standpoint of drawing ranges, however, it is necessary to consider only two basic types.

A ONE-PIECE RANGE

A one-piece range, called a **slide-in** or **drop-in range**, is a free-standing, conventional type of range that sits either on the floor or on a shallow, wooden base. It fits into the cabinetry to give a built-in look. The oven for this unit is usually below the range top. There are also models with the oven above the range top and others with ovens both above and below. **Figure 74** shows a one-piece range with the oven below.

SEPARATE COOKING TOPS AND WALL OVENS

A **cooking top** and a separate **built-in wall oven** make up another possible choice. With this arrangement, you can choose separate locations for each unit.

When a separate cooking top is used, it is installed in a cutout in the counter top with a base cabinet below. **Figure 75** illustrates a separate cooking top installed in a base cabinet.

The separate built-in or wall oven is installed in a special cabinet. It is usually located about counter height within the cabinet. Frequently, two ovens are used in this way, one above the other. **Figure 76** shows a typical separate oven installed in a cabinet.

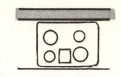

Figure 77. Average range sizes.

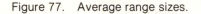

Figure 78. Symbol for range.

RANGE OR COOKING TOP SIZES

The first, 15 in. wide by 22 in. deep, is a small two-burner cooking top. It can be turned around and placed sideways in the counter if preferred.

The second, 30 in. wide by 22 in. deep, is an average-size four-burner range. It is the most commonly used type.

The third, 45 in. wide by 22 in. deep, is a four-burner range with a barbecue, grill, or combination of both, in the center.

The fourth, 45 in. wide by 22 in. deep, is an extra-large six-burner range. Refer to your design guides or **Fig. 77**.

DESIGNATING THE RANGE OR COOKING TOP ON THE PLAN:

1. Select the most suitable range and oven combination for your plan and decide where the units will be placed.
2. To draw either the one-piece range or the cooking top, select from the design guides on **Page 221**. See **Fig. 78**.
3. Trace your selection in the desired position.

WALL OVEN SIZES

Wall ovens are usually designed to be built into cabinets that are 24 in. wide. The measurement from the top of the oven to the bottom is determined by the make, model, and size one chooses. **Double-oven models** or **models with both a regular and an electronic oven** are usually manufactured with the ovens stacked one above the other. Consult manufacturers' literature for exact measurements.

TO DESIGNATE A SEPARATE WALL OVEN ON THE PLAN:

1. It is necessary only to indicate a wall oven by writing "Wall Oven" in the desired location.
2. When separate cabinets are made, the wall oven can be drawn in more detail. (See cabinets on **Page 80**.)

TO DESIGNATE A HOOD OR EXHAUST FAN ON THE PLAN:

1. A hood or exhaust fan over the range is designated by writing the words "Hood" or "Exhaust Fan" over the range as in **Fig. 84**.

REFRIGERATOR AND FREEZER SIZES

The two sizes of refrigerators or freezers given on the kitchen design guides are average-sized equipment. The larger refrigerator or freezer requires a space 36 in. wide by 28 in. deep. The small refrigerator or freezer requires a space 30 in. wide by 28 in. deep on the kitchen floor plan. (These sizes apply to the upright-type freezer.)

NOTE: Both the refrigerator and freezer project 3 to 4 in. beyond the counter top. They can be purchased with either right- or left-hand doors. Study your kitchen layout to determine which would work best. This door information does not have to be noted on the plan, except for your own reference. It is wise to allow at least 32 in., preferably 36 in., in width for this equipment when planning the cabinetry layout, even if the smaller size appliance has been chosen. At some future date, larger equipment might be desirable and it would not fit into the smaller space.

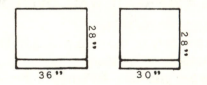

Figure 79. Symbol and sizes for refrigerator/or freezer.

TO DESIGNATE A REFRIGERATOR AND FREEZER ON THE PLAN:

1. The only designations necessary on the plan for refrigeration equipment are the units, their size, and the line of the cabinet above.
2. Refer to **Fig. 79** and to the refrigerator and/or freezer on the design guide.
3. Select the size that is to be used and trace it on your plan.

CABINETRY OVER THE REFRIGERATOR AND FREEZER

The refrigeration equipment can simply be fitted between base and wall cabinets. In some custom-cabinet designs, this equipment is built into cabinets to match the rest of the kitchen.

CABINETRY SIZES

There is room above the refrigerator and freezer for storage cabinets. Standard manufactured wall cabinets are 12 in. deep; however, they can be made the approximate depth of the refrigeration equipment. Deep cabinets in this location look better, provide additional storage space, and are much easier to reach.

DESIGNATING CABINETRY ON THE PLAN:

1. **Figure 84** shows the refrigerator drawn into the plan and the cabinet indicated with a dashed line above it.

DISHWASHER SIZES

While there are many different manufacturers of dishwashers, the basic size of nearly all makes and models is 24 in. in width. The depth is slightly less than 24 in. Most units are designed to be built into the 24-in. base cabinets and fit under the counter top. Portable models are also available. See **Fig. 80**.

NOTE: Most dishwasher doors are the full 24-in. width of the unit. They hinge at the bottom and open out into the room, taking up at least 20 in. of floor space.

The dishwasher is usually installed to either the right or the left of the sink and as close to it as possible.

In planning the location, consider the direction from which the dishes will be picked up, rinsed off, and placed in the dishwasher.

DESIGNATING THE DISHWASHER ON THE PLAN:

1. Refer to **Fig. 81** for the dishwasher designation.
2. When the dishwasher is located beneath the counter, it is indicated with two dashed lines, 24 in. apart, on the counter top. The letters **D/W** are written between the dashed lines.

Figure 80.   Dishwasher size.

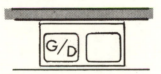

Figure 81.   Symbol for dishwasher.

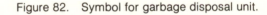
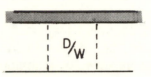

Figure 82.   Symbol for garbage disposal unit.

GARBAGE DISPOSAL UNITS

When using a double sink, choose carefully the side on which you wish to locate the garbage disposal unit. Dishes are usually scraped from left to right.

DESIGNATING GARBAGE DISPOSAL UNITS ON THE PLAN:

1. To designate a garbage disposal unit in either a single or double sink, write the letters **G/D** where the drain would be.
2. See **Fig. 82**.

SPECIAL KITCHEN EQUIPMENT

If there is to be any other special equipment in the kitchen, it is best to select it and get complete information in the form of literature from the manufacturer. This will help in your deciding where it is to be placed and tell you what the installation and mechanical requirements are.

TO DESIGNATE SPECIAL EQUIPMENT ON THE PLAN:

1. Write the name of the special equipment on the plan in the desired location and indicate the space requirement and any special electrical outlets or plumbing connections required.

CABINETS

Cabinets can be custom-made to meet your exact requirements, or they can be purchased ready-made from one of the many cabinet manufacturers.

CABINET SIZES

Manufactured cabinetry is available in many combinations of drawer and cabinet units which can be combined to fit your plan. Each is made in several sizes so that fitting units together to meet your space requirements can be done easily. Many cabinet manufacturers have developed designs for ingenious use of interior spaces.

The 24-in. deep cabinets beneath the counter are referred to as **base cabinets**. The narrower 12 in. cabinets above the counter are referred to as **wall cabinets**.

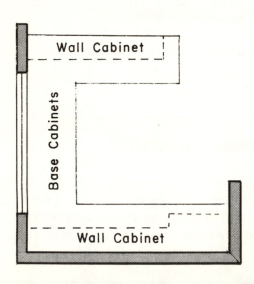

Figure 83. Plan showing base and wall cabinets.

DESIGNATING KITCHEN CABINETS ON THE PLAN:

1. In the first stages of kitchen planning, it was only necessary to indicate on the plan the area where the base and wall cabinets would be located. **Figure 71** on **Page 75** shows the first layout of a plan with the base cabinets indicated. **Figure 84** on **Page 81** shows the same plan with the wall cabinets added. Wall cabinets are usually indicated with a dashed line.
2. Now that the basic layout of the entire kitchen has been worked out satisfactorily, you can plan the details of the cabinetry more easily. Drawings of cabinet details are usually done on a separate plan which shows cabinet details only.
3. If you will be using manufactured cabinets, selections can be made and units planned to fit together from the detailed literature the manufacturer will supply. Many manufacturers have staff people who will help you to fit your selection of units into the plan.

KITCHEN COUNTER TOPS

When a **plastic laminate** (known under several brand names such as Formica) is used, a hole the size of the sink is cut out of the counter top. The sink fits into the hole and is trimmed with a metal rim.

Sinks are made especially for use with **tile**. They fit into a cutout in the supporting base. The tile is usually installed with special tile trim that fits over the edge of the sink, though there are other methods of installation suited to different sink designs.

Self-rimmed sinks are designed to be used with any of the foregoing counter tops. The sink is designed in such a way as to eliminate the need for a metal rim around the edge.

THE COMPLETED KITCHEN PLAN DRAWING

Figure 84 shows the symbols and designations for cabinets, sink, range, refrigerator, dishwasher, garbage disposal unit, and exhaust fan.

SELECTING AND DRAWING FOR THE LAUNDRY

Whether the plan is to have a separate laundry room, or to locate laundry equipment in a convenient area of the house, you will need to plan around basic laundry equipment sizes.

WASHING MACHINE AND DRYER SIZES

Washing machine and dryer sizes vary slightly. However, if the plan is to use the conventional large units (not the small portable type), a space approximately 60 in. wide is needed for the two units. This space allowance is a little larger than the appliances and is desirable, since it allows for moving the units in and out for servicing.

The appliances vary in depth approximately 27 to 30 in. Most models project 2 or 3 in. beyond the 24-in. base cabinets.

Laundry appliances are also made to be used beneath the counter. They fit within the 24-in. base-cabinet depth and allow for a continuous counter top. The doors open from the front.

TO DESIGNATE A WASHER AND DRYER ON THE PLAN:

1. Refer to the laundry appliances on the design guides and **Fig. 85**.
2. Trace them on your plan in the desired location.

TO DESIGNATE CABINETS ON THE PLAN:

1. Standard 12-in. wall cabinets over the washer and dryer are drawn with dashed line as shown in **Fig. 84**.

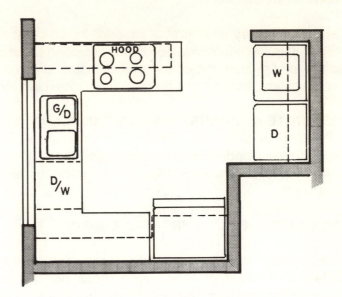

Figure 84.   Kitchen plan drawing.

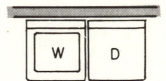

Figure 85.   Symbol for washing machine and dryer.

LAUNDRY SINK SIZES

The average laundry sink size is 20 x 22 in. Laundry sinks are usually deeper than kitchen sinks. Some are designed to be built into a base cabinet; others are hung on the wall or mounted on metal legs. These are convenient, especially if there is a separate laundry.

TO DESIGNATE A LAUNDRY SINK ON THE PLAN:

1. Refer to the laundry sink on the design guide for the laundry sink symbol as shown in **Fig. 86** and trace the sink on the plan.

TO DESIGNATE A BUILT-IN IRONING BOARD:

When an ironing board is built in, the entire unit fits into the wall and is enclosed with a door. The board drops down into correct position. The symbol for an ironing board is on the design guide sheet.

1. By tracing the symbol with a light dashed line, you can see how much space the board would take up in the room when opened into ironing position.
2. This symbol can also be used as a guide to space requirements for a portable ironing board.
3. See **Fig. 87**.

SELECTING AND DRAWING WATER HEATERS

There are two major types of water heaters used in homes: gas and electric.

Gas-burning water heaters have tall, narrow tanks. The burners are designed to burn either natural gas or liquid petroleum gas. They are available in several sizes but 30- or 40-gal. capacity models are often used in small to medium sized homes. The size and shape of each is given in **Fig. 88**.

Electrically heated water heaters have short, wide tanks. Some can be placed under counter tops or fitted into low places. They are available in several sizes. The average tank capacity is larger than that of the average gas water heater because electricity does not heat as quickly as gas. Average sizes and shapes are given in **Fig. 89**.

TO DESIGNATE A WATER HEATER ON THE PLAN:

1. The symbol for drawing either type of water heater is a circle the same size as the heater, marked **w/h**, as shown in **Fig. 90**.

Figure 86.   Laundry sink.

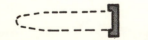

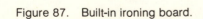

Figure 87.   Built-in ironing board.

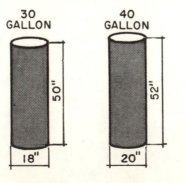

Figure 88.   Gas water heater sizes.

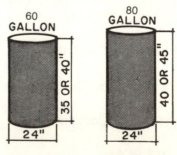

Figure 89.   Electric water heater sizes.

Figure 90.
Symbol for water heater.

SELECTING AND DRAWING HEATING AND COOLING EQUIPMENT

Heating and cooling equipment is available in many sizes and types. The equipment selected should supply sufficient heating and cooling so that the home is adequately warm during the coldest day and comfortably cool during the hottest.

The choice of heating and cooling equipment must be based on the type of fuel to be used. Investigate the availability and cost of fuel in your area before the selection is made.

NOTE: In the preliminary stages of plan drawing, it is only necessary to determine the type of equipment to be used so that you can allow space on your plan for it.

GAS WALL FURNACES

There are simple and economical furnaces available which are built into the wall and do not take up floor space. These furnaces burn either natural gas or liquid petroleum gas. They are usually located in halls, so that the heat can circulate throughout the house.

LARGER-SIZED FURNACES

There are many makes, models, and types of larger-sized furnaces. They are usually installed in a centrally located closet especially built to house them. Heating and cooling units are frequently combined in this type of unit.

COAL- OR OIL-BURNING FURNACES

Coal and oil-burning furnaces are available in areas where conditions warrant their use.

NOTE: If the plan is to have a basement, it is an ideal place to locate a furnace.

ELECTRIC WALL HEATERS

This type of heater is sometimes called a space heater and is built into the wall. Several individual units are usually located throughout the house.

AIR CONDITIONING UNITS

Heating and air conditioning units are often combined in one piece of equipment, though many types of individual cooling units are available. The dual-type installation saves floor space.

Because heating and cooling are complex subjects, it is advisable to consult with local dealers who supply the "heat loss calculations" which are required by most building departments. Heat loss calculations are figures which determine the size of the equipment needed. These figures are based on the size of the house, window area, insulation, weather conditions, etc.

DESIGNATING HEATING AND COOLING UNITS ON THE PLAN:

1. The average size of a gas wall furnace and the designation for drawing it are shown in **Fig. 91**.
2. **Figure 92** shows the average size and designation for drawing electric wall heaters.
3. **Figure 93** shows the designation for drawing larger-sized furnaces.
4. **Figure 94** shows the designation to use when indicating a coal- or oil-burning furnace. The space allowed on the plan for a furnace will depend upon the size and type of furnace.

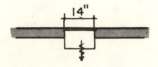

Figure 91.   Gas wall furnace.

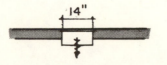

Figure 92.   Electric wall heater.

Figure 93.
Larger-sized furnace.

Figure 94.   Coal- or oil-burning furnace.

83

SELECTING INSULATION

Insulation is used to hold heated air *in* during winter months and to keep heat *out* during summer months. A well insulated house is much more energy efficient and comfortable to live in.

Insulating while a new home or an addition is under construction is desirable because it can be done more efficiently and at less cost. However, insulation can be installed in existing homes.

The attic ranks first in importance, but all exterior walls should be insulated as well. One can prevent further heat loss by insulating basement walls, under floors, and other areas where cold air can penetrate.

There are many kinds of insulation. The type and grade selected should be determined by the method of construction employed and local weather conditions.

NOTE: Check with the local building department for regulations pertaining to insulation.

TO DESIGNATE INSULATION ON THE PLAN:

1. Determine the most suitable specifications for insulating the home by checking with insulation manufacturers in your area or by reading manufacturers' literature.
2. Verify your finding with the local building department.
3. Write instructions for installation on the plan in the form of a note.
4. This note, along with other pertinent information, should appear in a conspicuous place beside the floor plan on the "Floor Plan Page" of your set of drawings.

SELECTING AND DRAWING FIREPLACES

There are suitable fireplace designs for every floor plan. The number of styles, combined with the large selection of interesting brick, stone, and other materials suitable for fireplace construction and finish, is almost unlimited.

The fireplace designs given on the design guides, and shown in **Figures 95** and **95a**, are examples of typical shapes and sizes. The sizes are average and can vary, depending on ones' requirements and the local building code.

FIREPLACE NO. 1

This is the most commonly used style. It is a popular design for several reasons. It is economical and easy to build, and it does an excellent job of heating. A 36-in. front opening is typical of those used in the average home. However, the front opening (or firebox) is often 40 or 42 in. wide to allow for larger logs. If this fireplace is located on an outside wall, it takes up very little space in the room, as most of the masonry can be installed on the outside of the house.

FIREPLACE NO. 2

This is a design which fits into the corner of a room. The front and one end are open, allowing a view of the fire from two sides. It is very attractive in an appropriate location. In this design, most of the fireplace and a continuous hearth on two sides project into the room. The firebox is usually approximately 42 in. wide by about 30 in. deep, though sizes vary.

FIREPLACE NO. 3

This is a design suitable for use between rooms. It is open at the front and at the back. With this design, it is necessary to build only one fire to heat two rooms. Each room appears to have its own fireplace. It takes the full width and depth of the fireplace plus two hearths out of the floor space. The firebox is usually about 40 in. wide by 30 in. deep.

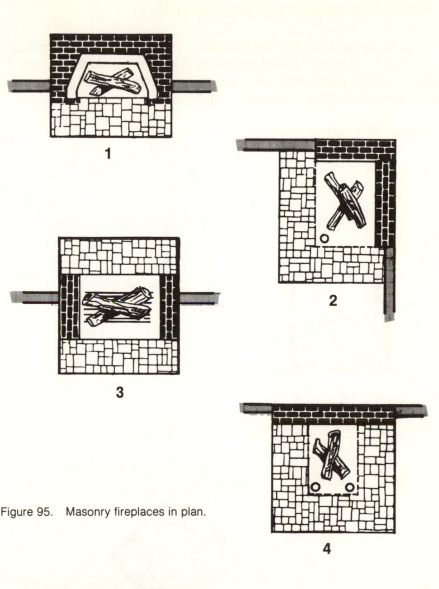

Figure 95.   Masonry fireplaces in plan.

FIREPLACE NO. 4

This style is open on the front and both sides. It is very effective when located properly since one can see the fire from all three sides. Almost the entire fireplace projects into the room, besides a continuous hearth on three sides. The firebox is usually about 36 in. wide by 24 in. deep.

FIREPLACE NO. 5

This is an example of a free-standing, pre-fabricated unit mounted on a base of a fireproof material such as brick, tile, or asbestos board. These fireplaces come from the manufacturer completely finished and are available in many sizes, shapes, and colors.

FIREPLACE NO. 6

This style is a one-piece hood over a masonry fire pit.

5

Figure 95a.   Prefabricated fireplaces in plan.

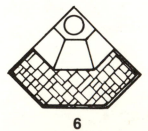

6

TO DESIGNATE A FIREPLACE ON THE PLAN:

1. Select from the fireplace designs and draw the fireplace on the plan according to the following instructions:
2. Decide on its location and where it will fit, in relation to the walls. The shaded lines which extend from the fireplace in **Fig. 95** represent walls.
3. Trace the selected fireplace on the plan from the design guides.
4. Where possible a **cleanout** for ashes is desirable. Indicate as shown in **Fig. 99**.
5. Pipe is frequently installed through the masonry to provide a **gas log lighter**, indicated as shown in **Fig. 99**.

NOTE: Hearth requirements are a minimum of 18 in. in depth, as illustrated in Fig. 95.

PLACEMENT AND INSTALLATION OF FIREPLACES

The usual procedure for installing **Fireplace No. 1**, is to allow 4 in. (one-brick thickness) to project into the room as in **Fig. 95**. However, the walls and masonry can intersect at any point desired.

Fireplaces No. 2 and 4 fit into the wall as shown in **Fig. 95**.

The walls intersecting **Fireplace No. 3** do not have to be centered on the masonry. Cabinets or walls can be used on either or both sides in whatever location desired.

The use of **Fireplace No. 5** allows much more flexibility. These fireplaces can be placed almost anywhere in the room. There are only two requirements: a pipe through the roof surrounded by non-heat-conducting material and a base of some noncombustible material, such as brick or tile. If the unit is installed close to a wall, non-combustible material is usually installed on the wall.

Fireplace No. 6 is typical of prefabricated hoods that can be used over masonry or metal fire pits.

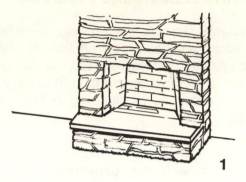

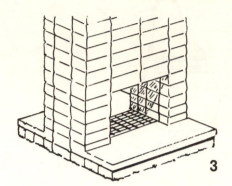

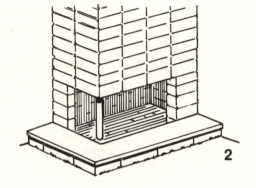

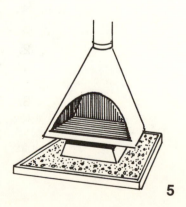

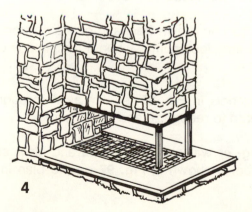

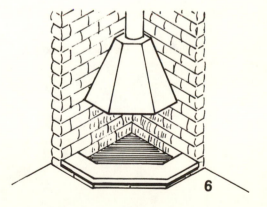

1

2

3

4

5

6

Figure 96.   Pictorial drawings of the fireplaces in Figures 95 and 95a and on the design guides.

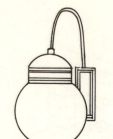

A

SYMBOL FOR
WALL—MOUNT
LIGHT FIXTURE

B

SYMBOL FOR
CEILING LIGHT FIXTURE

Figure 97.   Electrical symbols.

SELECTING AND DESIGNATING ELECTRICAL SYMBOLS

In the drawing plans system, symbols for lighting, switches, outlets, telephones, and televisions are not drawn on the plan until after the furniture arrangement has been worked out and the swing of the doors planned. With the furniture drawn on the plan, it is easy to lay out the electrical work, as you can see by referring to **Fig. 112**, **Page 112**, and **Fig. 99**, **Page 92**.

Your local building department will require that the house be wired according to code. Check with the department for the requirements in your area.

The electrician who wires the house will have no way of knowing how the rooms will be used unless electrical symbols are clearly drawn on the plan.

Careless planning results in outlets behind heavy furniture, none where they are needed, and occasionally a switch behind a door.

DESIGNATING ELECTRICAL SYMBOLS ON THE PLAN:

1.   Electrical symbols can be drawn freehand or traced from the design guides, but they look neater when a template is used for drawing circles.

2.   By copying the symbols in **Fig. 97**, shown as **A** through **H**, you can quickly learn to recognize and draw them.

3.   Select either **ceiling- or wall-mounted lights** and draw either symbol **A** or symbol **B** shown in **Fig. 97** on the plan in the location chosen.

4. Indicate **light switches** with the symbol marked **C**. To clarify which switch turns on which light, connect the switch to the light with a curved, dashed line. If the switch chosen will activate an outlet, simply dash a curved line from the switch to the outlet. Refer to the floor plan in **Fig. 99** and to **Fig. 112**.

5. The symbol marked **D** is used to designate **outlets**. One symbol is marked 110. It has two lines through it. This is the symbol used for ordinary household current. The other is marked 220; it has three lines through it. It is used for appliances which require 220 volts, such as electric stoves and clothes dryers.

6. Wiring and outlets for the **telephone** are usually provided by the telephone company during the course of construction. Indicate the location preferred by drawing the symbol marked **E.**

7. **Television antenna lead-in wires** are generally placed in the walls during the course of construction. When the decision has been made for the location of the television set, draw the symbol marked **F** on the plan.

8. **Electric heat, light and ventilation for the bathrooms** can be provided by installing a combination unit in the ceiling. A special switch or dial enables the user to select heat circulation by a blower fan, light, and exhaust fan or any combination of two. To designate this type of fixture, use the symbol marked **G** and specify "combination unit". The same symbol may be used to indicate a built-in radiant ceiling heater with fan or light.

9. The symbol marked **H** designates a **ceiling fan** which is used to exhaust air out of areas requiring additional ventilation.

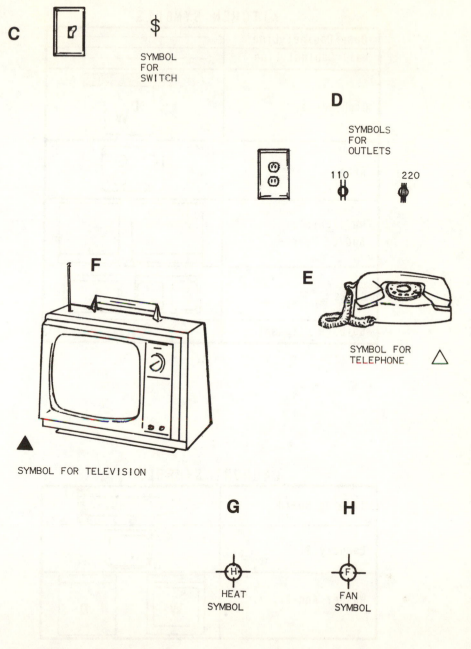

C $
SYMBOL FOR SWITCH

D
SYMBOLS FOR OUTLETS
110   220

F

E
SYMBOL FOR TELEPHONE

SYMBOL FOR TELEVISION

G
HEAT SYMBOL

H
FAN SYMBOL

Figure 97a. Electrical Symbols

QUICK REFERENCE SYMBOL CHART

KITCHEN SYMBOLS

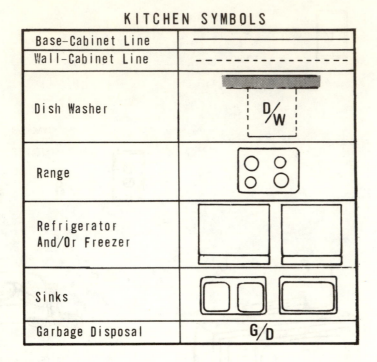

Base-Cabinet Line	————————
Wall-Cabinet Line	– – – – – – –
Dish Washer	D/W
Range	
Refrigerator And/Or Freezer	
Sinks	
Garbage Disposal	G/D

LAUNDRY SYMBOLS

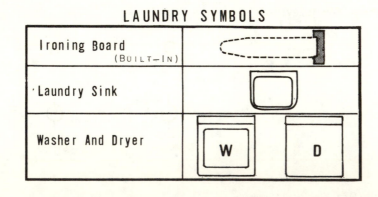

Ironing Board (BUILT-IN)	
Laundry Sink	
Washer And Dryer	W D

BATHROOM SYMBOLS

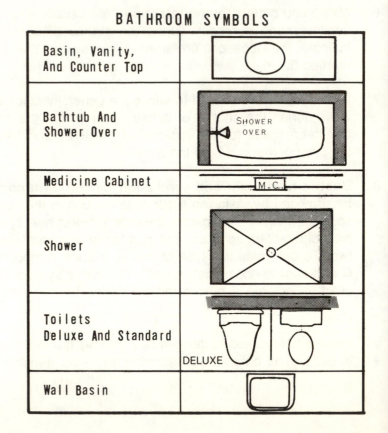

Basin, Vanity, And Counter Top	
Bathtub And Shower Over	SHOWER OVER
Medicine Cabinet	M.C.
Shower	
Toilets Deluxe And Standard	DELUXE
Wall Basin	

Figure 98.   Quick reference chart.

WATER HEATER SYMBOL

Water Heater	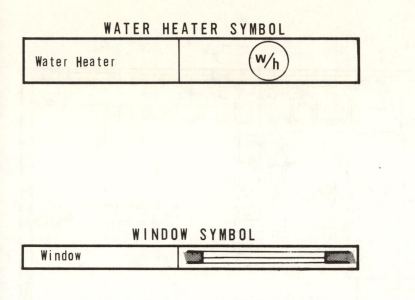

WINDOW SYMBOL

Window	

DOOR SYMBOLS

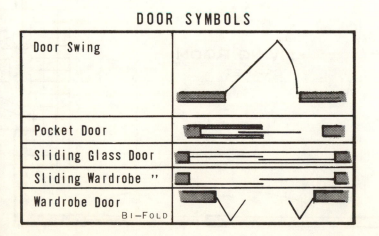

Door Swing	
Pocket Door	
Sliding Glass Door	
Sliding Wardrobe "	
Wardrobe Door BI-FOLD	

ELECTRICAL SYMBOLS

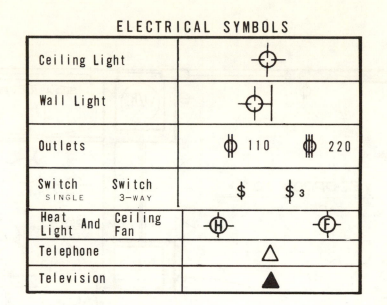

Ceiling Light	
Wall Light	
Outlets	110 220
Switch SINGLE Switch 3-WAY	$ $3
Heat Light And Ceiling Fan	H F
Telephone	△
Television	▲

FIREPLACE SYMBOLS

For Symbols	SEE PAGES 85 AND 86.

HEATING AND COOLING SYMBOLS

For Symbols	SEE PAGE 83

91

Figure 98a.   Quick reference chart.

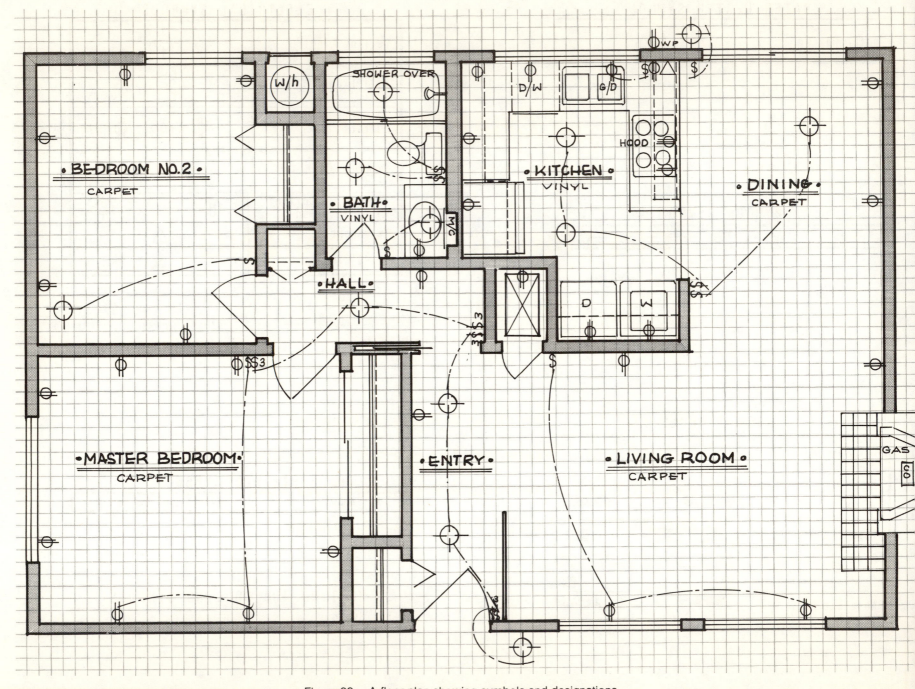

Figure 99. A floor plan showing symbols and designations.

CHAPTER SIX

PRELIMINARY PLANNING

PLANNING

DIAGRAM

MAKING A PLANNING DIAGRAM

A planning diagram is a rough sketch, usually composed of circular shapes representing the various living areas in a home, arranged on a plan of a lot (plot plan). The reason for drawing a planning diagram is to study the relationship of the various living areas to each other, to the lot, and to the sun.

In **Figure 100**, a planning diagram has been drawn on a plot plan so that the available space for the house and the way it relates to the lot can be analyzed.

AREAS OF ACTIVITY

The floor space in every home can be divided into several main areas of activity such as food preparation and dining, sleeping, and living. Bathrooms, entry and halls, laundry, storage, and car shelter can be considered, for planning purposes, as secondary areas.

THE VALUE OF A PLANNING DIAGRAM

Drawing a planning diagram gives one an opportunity to consider all of the factors involved before committing to a set floor plan. It can save a great deal of time and serve as a guide and a reminder when you draw a floor plan. Design professionals frequently make numerous sketches and diagrams at this stage of plan development, taking into account every known factor and circumstance of the lot as well as the needs and requirements of the individuals who will live in the home.

PLANNING FOR AN ADDITION

If you have drawn a plot plan that shows the existing house, garage, driveway, etc., a planning diagram will help you to visualize the available space on the lot for the addition, the orientation of the windows of the addition to the sun, and the relationship of the new space to the existing space.

PLANNING FOR A REMODELING PROJECT

It is easier, on a planning diagram, to see how the desired changes will effect the over-all space arrangement, traffic paths, and the interrelationship of one area of activity to another and to the environment of the setting.

PLANNING FOR A NEW HOME

The information given in **Project 11** will help you formulate some ideas for the arrangement of primary living areas and the best shape of the house as it relates to the setting.

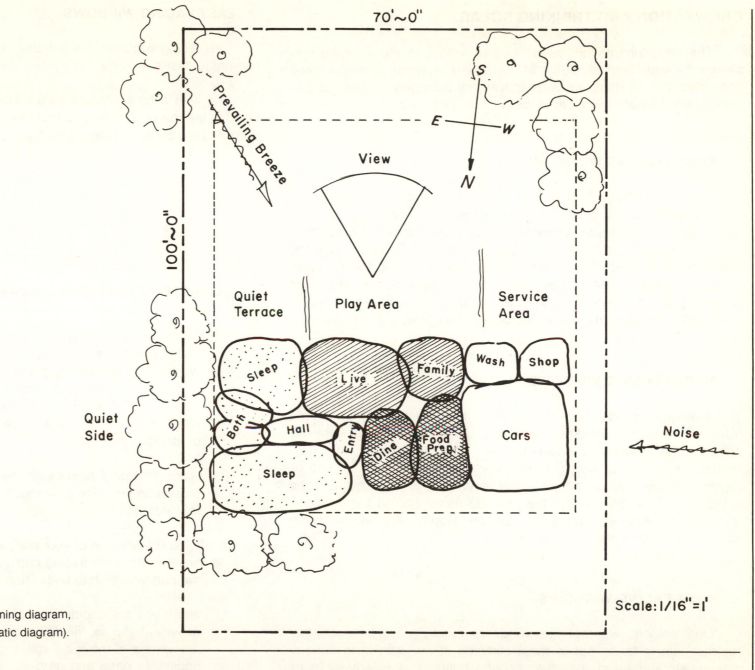

Figure 100.   An example of a planning diagram,
(sometimes called a schematic diagram).

ORIENTATION AND THINKING SOLAR

The word orientation, as used here, refers to the way the sun strikes the walls and windows of the house. A home is much more comfortable if the main areas of activity are arranged so that the sun shines into the right windows at the right time of the day.

SOUTH FACING WINDOWS

Maximum utilization of the sun, to warm the house in the winter, can be achieved by orienting major living areas so windows face *south*. Rooms with *south* facing windows will be warmer and easier to heat and they will be flooded with sunlight most of the day during the winter months. *South* facing windows will be shaded in the summer, when the angle of the sun is higher, if the house has a fairly wide overhang on the *south* side. Kitchens and family rooms are usually occupied in the daytime and would benefit from a southern exposure.

NORTH FACING WINDOWS

Although rooms facing *north* receive little direct sunlight, the light from *north* facing windows provides excellent working light for projects that require consistent, even light throughout the day. Bedrooms with *north* facing windows would be desirable for late or daytime sleepers because they would receive very little sunlight. If the living room is to be used in the evening more than in the daytime, *north* facing windows might be suitable. Rooms with *north* facing windows will be cooler in the summer.

WEST FACING WINDOWS

One seldom wants large windows facing *west* because the summer sun is far to hot in most climates. If the plan is to have a garage, storage room, or other service building, it is advisable to place it on the *west* side to serve as a buffer between the sun and the *west* wall of the house.

EAST FACING WINDOWS

East facing windows are suitable in rooms where early morning sunlight is desired.

Orienting a house to the best advantage is not difficult and the benefits are many. A little time invested in observing the way the sun casts its rays on the lot can reward you with amazing dividends.

TO SKETCH A PLANNING DIAGRAM:

1. Cover the plot plan you have drawn with tracing paper, making sure it is taped securely to your drawing surface. By working on the tracing paper, you can experiment with and discard ideas until you find a tentative arrangement of the main areas of activity that meets your requirements. In this way the plot plan stays clean and does not have to be continuously redrawn.

2. Make as many studies as necessary. Try different house shapes and main area arrangements. Keep all of your sketches for reference.

3. If you like one part of your planning diagram but wish to change another, lay fresh tracing paper over the first sketch and copy the part you wish to use. Then draw in the new part.

4. When you are deciding on the best arrangement of areas of activity, keep in mind the available space on the lot, the relationship of the living space to the driveway and car shelter, access to patio and garden, privacy, and orientation to the sun. Some other factors to consider are noise, view, and prevailing breeze.

PRELIMINARY FLOOR PLANS

In preparing floor plans, the first drawing to be made is called a preliminary floor plan. A preliminary floor plan is a drawing that reflects your first ideas of the way the house space will be arranged.

When you have drawn a plot plan from the book example or a project of your own, and made a planning diagram, you will have done some of the preparatory work for drawing your preliminary floor plan.

PROJECT 12   **Preparing To Sketch A Preliminary Floor Plan**

Objective: *To assemble and evaluate the plot plans and the planning diagrams you have drawn in preparation for actually drawing a preliminary floor plan.*

Materials Required: *All drawings, notes, sketches, and lists you have made up to this point in the planning*

LISTING PREFERENCES:

1. **"Do Wants"**   You may find it useful to make a list of all the things wanted in a home. List the number of bedrooms and the approximate size of each. List each of the other rooms needed and their approximate sizes. List special features the home should have, such as a family room opening to the patio as well as the kitchen, or a retreat for quiet activities.

2. **"Don't Wants"**   A "don't want" list might serve a useful purpose also, such as "don't want" people walking through the kitchen to get to other rooms, "don't want" children using the front entrance when coming in from play, etc.

3. **Thinking Solar**   In deciding on the location and arrangement of rooms, you should consider the direction of the sun. List the rooms in which morning sun is desirable and those in which morning sun is not desirable. Consider the effect afternoon sun will have on each room in the summer and in the winter. If you live in a hot climate, select a location for a patio that can be served from the kitchen conveniently and that is in the shade on late summer afternoons.

4. **Make Lists**   Your list of the furnishings and appliances to be used in the new home and their sizes will serve to remind you of the items that must be fitted into the plan. See **Fig. 105** on **Page 105**.

PROJECT 13   Sketching A Preliminary Floor Plan

Objective: *To sketch your floor-plan ideas in an approximate scale, drawing, revising, and discarding, until you have produced a plan with which you are reasonably satisfied.*

Materials Required: *The 1/4-in. scale ruler from Page 229, design guides from Pages 215-227, larger sheets of squared drawing paper (about 18 x 24 inches) tracing paper equal in size to the squared drawing paper, pencil, eraser, drafting tape*

TO SKETCH A PRELIMINARY PLAN:

Preliminary plans are usually drawn to a scale in which 1/8 in. = 1 ft. However, since the final working drawing is done in 1/4-in. scale, it is suggested that you draw your preliminary plan in the scale of 1/4 in. = 1 ft.

1. Fasten a sheet of squared drawing paper to your drawing surface and cover it with a piece of tracing paper, taped firmly in place.

2. With your planning diagram, plot plan, and any sketched ideas you may have before you, proceed to work out a preliminary floor plan in scale.

3. Draw a line to represent the approximate exterior shape you have worked out on the plot plan. Make your drawings as nearly correct in size as you are able to in this beginning stage.

4. Draw a second line, 6 in. *in* from the first one, to represent the wall thickness.

5. Lay out interior partitions tentatively, dividing the space within the boundaries of the exterior walls into rooms. Use two lines 6 in. apart to represent wall thickness.

6. Each time you wish to begin a new concept, fasten a fresh piece of tracing paper over the first one and redraw, copying the parts you are satisfied with and making the necessary changes.

7. You may draw and discard plans on tracing paper many times before your plan begins to satisfy your requirements and make the best use of the lot space. This stage of the drawing requires patience and perseverance. Avoid the pitfall of clinging to your first ideas, because first ideas can always be improved upon. Keep an open mind.

8. The following details should be included on your preliminary plans:

    (a) Correct closet depths: 2 ft. - 8 in., including both front and back walls is the minimum practical depth.

    (b) Correct size and space allowances for bathroom and kitchen fixtures, appliances and cabinetry. See **Pages 71-82**.

9. During the process of working out a floor plan, it will be helpful to study the plans in this book and any others that are available to you.

10. A preliminary plan represents your first thinking and you will make many changes before completing it. It is a creative study, made to determine the best possible use of the space available to you. Consequently, electrical and mechanical details do not appear on the preliminary plan. They will be worked out when the working drawings are being prepared.

11. For furniture planning see **Project 15** "How To Draw Room Studies" beginning on **Page 102**.

SQUARE FOOTAGE MEANS AREA OF FLOOR SPACE

The cost of a house is determined by its size and the type and quality of the construction materials specified.

When your first tentative exterior walls have been drawn, it is important for you to know the square footage of the house you have laid out. Each time you change the size and shape of an exterior wall, figure the square footage again so that you will know the size of the house you are drawing at all times.

When figuring square footage, always keep the figures for the house and the garage separate. There is considerable cost difference between the two.

DETERMINING SQUARE FOOTAGE :

1. If a house is square or rectangular, such as the plan in **Fig. 102** which measures 24 ft. x 36 ft., you simply multiply 24 x 36, which equals 864. Consequently there are 864 square feet of floor space in the plan.

2. If you are figuring the square footage in a house that has angles and offsets such as the plan in **Fig. 101**, you mark the areas off into squares or rectangles and multiply the width times the length of each area of the house. When you have the square footage for each area, add them all together. Refer to **Fig. 101**.

   NOTE: The symbol ☞ is often used to indicate square feet.

House area	A	60 ft. x 24 ft. =	1,440 sq. ft.
	B	10 ft. x 28 ft. =	280
	C	16 ft. x 24 ft. =	384
			2,104 sq. ft.
Garage area		20 ft. x 20 ft. =	400 sq. ft.

PROJECT 14   How To Figure Square Footage

Objective: *To learn how to measure a scale drawing of a room, a house, a lot, or any given area in order to determine how many square feet it contains. These figures are needed when determining cost, figuring building material requirements, and judging the size of mechanical equipment needed, such as heating and cooling apparatus.*

Materials Required: *The 1/4-in. scale ruler from Page 229, your preliminary floor plan with exterior measurements, pencil, scratch paper*

Figure 101.   Figuring square footage.

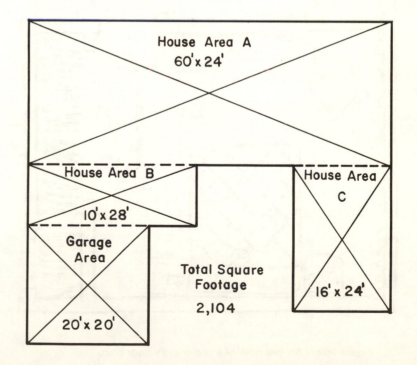

House Area A
60' x 24'

House Area B

House Area C

10' x 28'

Garage Area

Total Square Footage
2,104

16' x 24'

20' x 20'

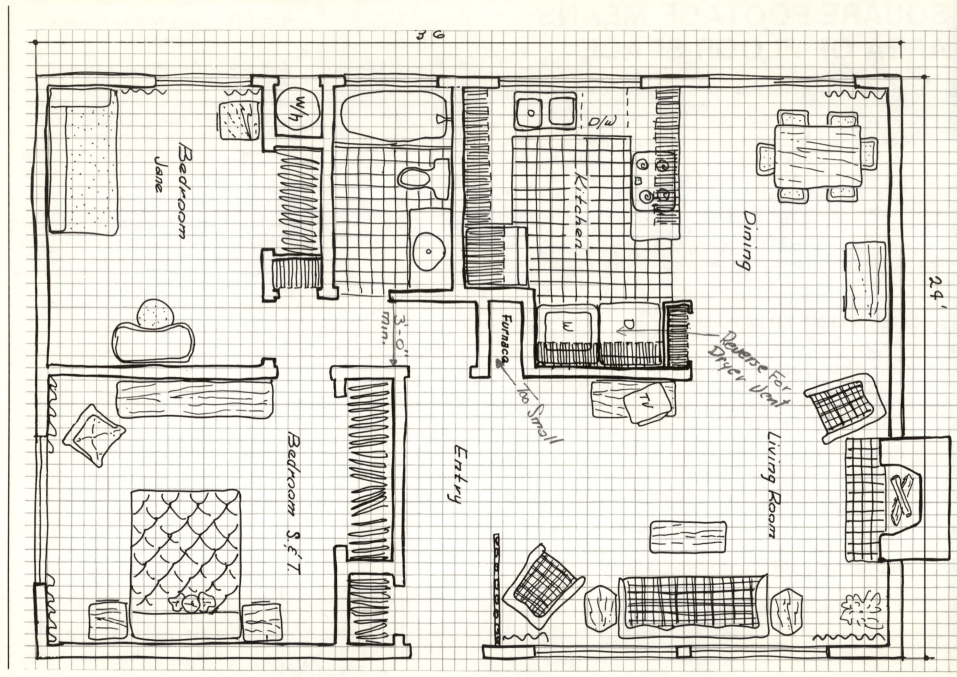

Figure 102.   An example of a preliminary floor plan.

CHAPTER SEVEN

DRAWING ROOM STUDIES
FROM PRELIMINARY PLANS

PROJECT 15   How To Draw Room Studies

PROJECT 15   How To Draw Room Studies

Objective: *To make studies of each of the rooms of the plan. These studies will reveal the most suitable location for doors, windows, furniture, electrical outlets, cabinetry, etc.*

Materials Required: *Design guides and 1/4-in scale ruler from Pages 215 to 229, squared drawing paper*

For remodeling or rearranging: A 1/4-in. scale drawing of each room you plan to revise, (see Page 33) drawn on squared drawing paper, a list of sizes of each piece of furniture or equipment to be used in each room, small tracing paper, pencil, eraser, colored pencil, drafting tape

For a new home or an addition: Your preliminary plan, notes, evaluation list, list of furniture measurements, small sheets of tracing paper, pencil, eraser, colored pencil, drafting tape

ROOM STUDIES

DRAWING ROOM STUDIES FROM PRELIMINARY PLANS

When a preliminary plan has been completed, the planning has progressed to the point where it is possible to make careful studies of each of the rooms in your floor plan. The purpose of these studies is to reveal the most advantageous placement of such things as doors, windows, cabinetry, plumbing fixtures, light fixtures, and electrical outlets.

MAKING AN EVALUATION LIST

This is a good time to evaluate the ways in which each room will be used. This can be done by listing all of the activities that will take place in each room. When you are sure about how the room will be used and by whom, your drawing will progress more easily.

MEASURING AND LISTING FURNISHINGS AND EQUIPMENT

Drawing furniture and other necessary equipment on the plan will help you to visualize the available space and determine the best way to use it. If presently owned furniture is to be used, obtain the measurements. It will save time if the height, width, and depth of each piece is measured and the figures kept in a notebook for handy reference. If all new furniture will be used, you can plan attractive, functional rooms by selecting furniture from the design guides. If corresponding items on the design guides are not exactly the same size as the pieces to be used, you can adjust them with the help of the scale ruler.

The secret of good planning is in keeping the plan flexible until you have completed studies for each room. You may draw and discard numerous room studies before arriving at the one with which you are completely satisfied. As you continue to draw and study one room after the other, you may begin to change your mind about some of your first drawings and go back to revise them. For this reason it is only necessary to make sketches, accurate enough to show details clearly. Many quick studies will prove to be more useful than one or two laboriously done drawings.

By the time you have completed the room studies, you will have eliminated most of the flaws in the design. It is much easier and less costly to draw, change, and throw away paper, than it is to knock out walls to make changes after construction has begun.

TO DRAW A ROOM STUDY:

1. Select a room from your preliminary plan for your first room study, preferably an easy one to draw, like the living room. Keep your preliminary plan, notebook of furniture measurements, and evaluation list handy for reference.

2. Fasten squared paper from the kit to your drawing surface. If you are planning a room that is rectangular, lay out the plan with the long measurement on the widest side of the paper. Draw the walls of the room plan, then cover the drawing with tracing paper.

3. Tentatively lay out the room you are planning on squared drawing paper. Use light pressure on a well-pointed lead.

STEP 1

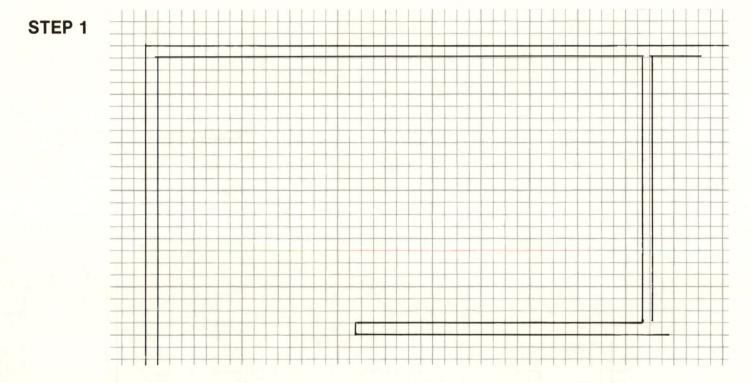

Figure 103.

NOTE: This example study of the living room was taken from the actual floor plan, Fig. 13, Page 29.

4. Decide on a tentative placement for windows and door openings. Draw the windows according to your preliminary plan. Erase spaces for door openings.

STEP 2

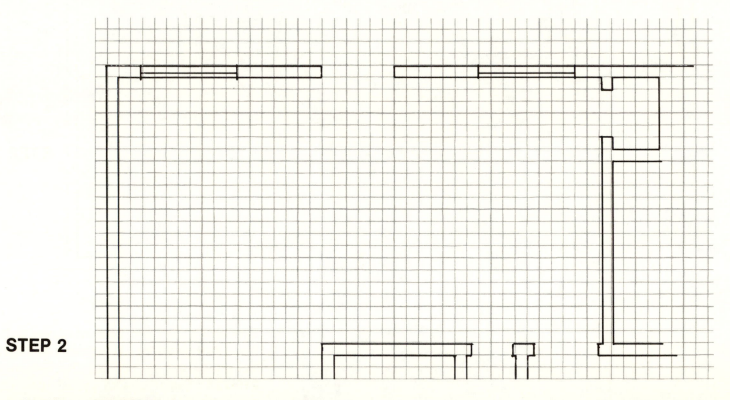

Figure 104.

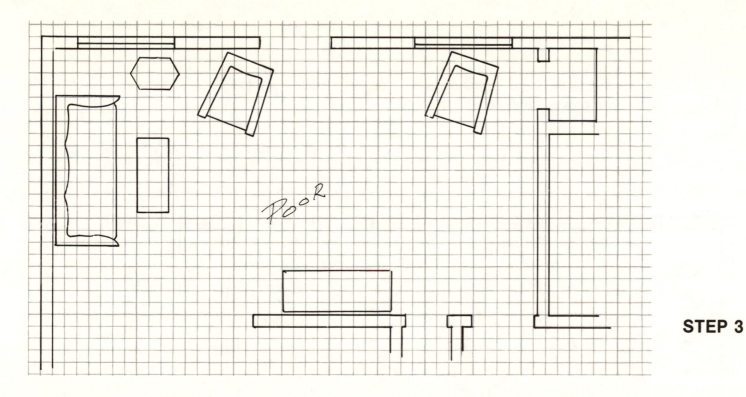

POOR

Figure 105.

STEP 3

5. Tentatively plan and draw whatever furnishings or equipment the room requires. Wherever appropriate, trace from the design guides or cut out the required items from **Pages 215-227**. These cut-out pieces can be moved around on the plan until a desirable arrangement is found. If the room is to have a fireplace or other feature, keep this in mind.

6. Relocate the door openings and windows as necessary for an improved furniture arrangement.

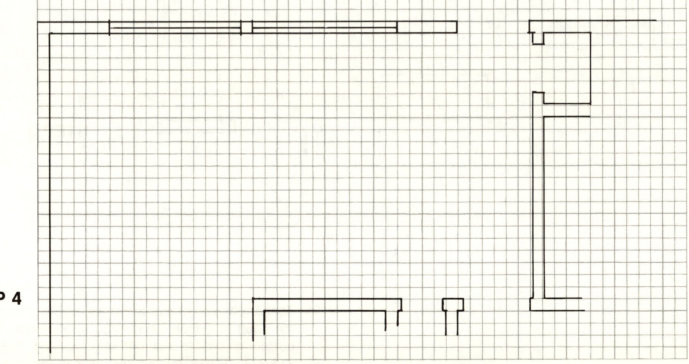

STEP 4

Figure 106.

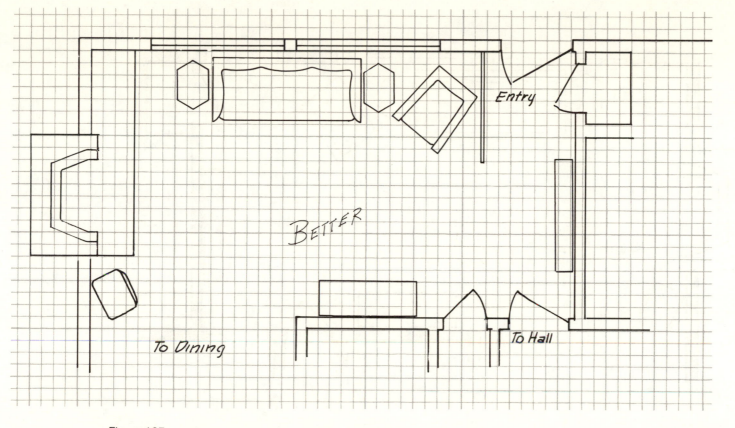

Better

Entry

To Dining

To Hall

Figure 107.

7. When you are satisfied with your arrangement of doors, windows, and furniture, draw in the door swings so that you can determine whether or not open doors conflict with the furniture arrangement - as does the door leading to the hall in **Fig. 107**. If a fireplace is to be added, select a design from the drawing guide and draw it in the chosen location. Keep in mind the relationship of this room to the rest of the plan.

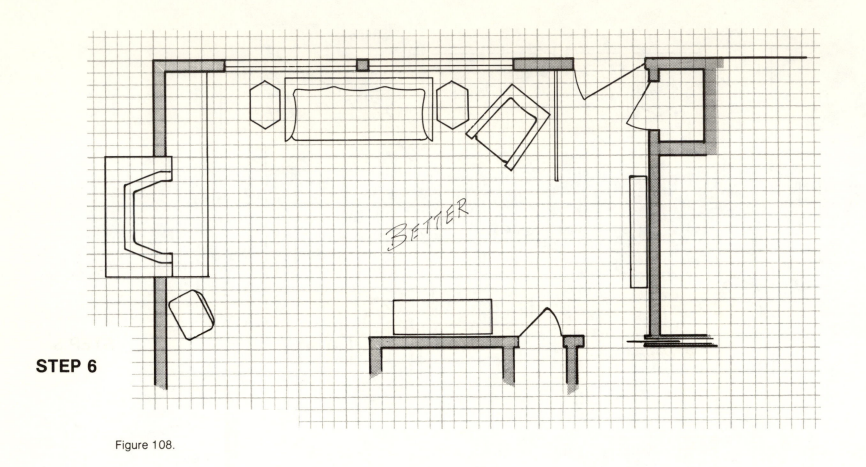

STEP 6

Figure 108.

8. Go over lines that represent walls with a heavier pressure on your well-pointed lead or with a softer lead. The walls will be more clearly defined if they are shaded with a colored pencil.

9. Wherever drapes will take up wall space they should be planned for. Decide on the direction the drapes will pull and draw them on the plan. Drapes that are hung on a single track will take up about 6 in. of floor space, as shown in **Fig. 109**. At least 10 in. of depth is required for overdrapes on a double rod. Note that the fireplace hearth has been cut back to permit the drapes to draw all the way to the corner.

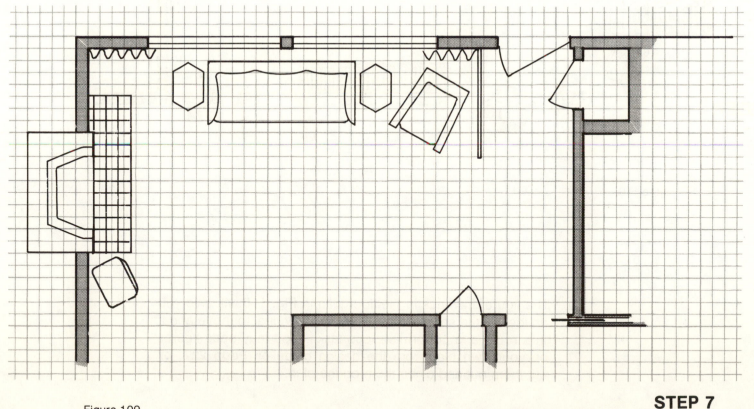

Figure 109.

STEP 7

STEP 8

Figure 110.

10. The figure drawings in the floor plan in **Fig. 110** will give you an idea of the space required for an individual to move about in a room and perform various tasks. You may trace figures on your own plan from the design guide on **Page 227**, or cut them out and place them on the plan.

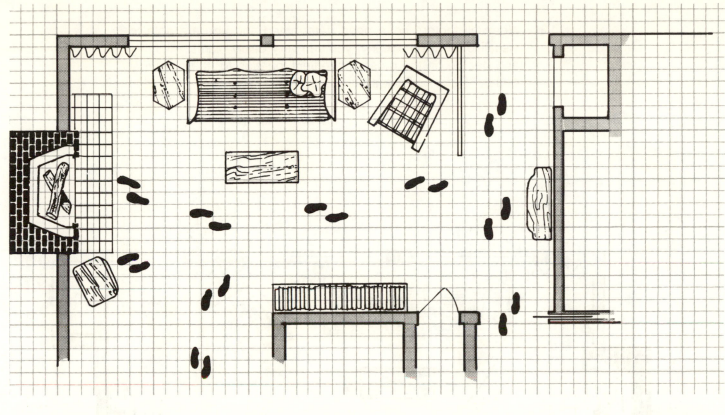

Figure 111.

11. The footsteps in the drawing in **Fig. 111** show the pattern most traffic will take through the room. Consider the way people will walk through the room you are planning, to be sure there is no conflict with your furniture.

12. When all factors have been determined and you are able to visualize the room clearly, you can very easily plan the lighting and decide on the most convenient location for the electrical outlets. Refer to **Pages 88-89**.

STEP 10

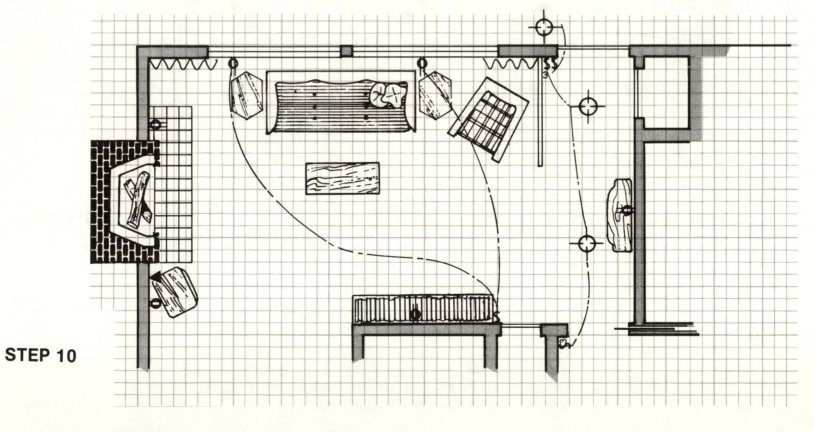

Figure 112.

CHAPTER EIGHT

PLANNING VEHICLE AREAS

PROJECT 16   **Things To Consider When Planning
A Garage Or Carport**

PROJECT 16 **Things To Consider When Planning A Garage Or Carport**

Objective: *To plan a garage so that maximum use is made of the available space. This can be achieved by carefully planning the placement of doors, windows, parking-space allowances, and other facilities.*

Materials Required: *A 1/4-in. scale ruler, drawing guides, squared drawing paper, your preliminary garage plan, list of items you plan to put in the garage and the size of each, pencil, eraser, colored pencil, drafting tape*

VEHICLE AREAS

Accurate planning for garages, carports, driveways, and parking space is essential. Whether or not the plan is to build a garage or carport at the same time as the house is built, these facilities should be provided for in the original planning.

The average garage or carport is built according to the following list of minimum sizes:

2-Car garage or carport	Minimum width	18 ft.-4 in.
	Minimum length	20 ft.-0 in.
1-Car garage or carport	Minimum width	10 ft.-0 in.
	Minimum length	20 ft.-0 in.

The foregoing figures are inside wall measurements taken between framed walls or carport posts, as shown in **Fig. 113-115.** This garage size information was taken from *Minimum Property Standards*, a book issued by the Federal Housing Administration.

CAR SHELTERS

Car shelters built according to these specifications will accommodate the number of vehicles they are designed for, but have inadequate space for storage or activities. Since garage space is less expensive to build than house space, it is desirable to add two to three additional feet to your garage plan, either in length or width, where lot space permits.

PLANNING THE GARAGE:

1. At least one window is desirable in the garage for light and ventilation.

2. A door leading to the service yard or garden is convenient.

3. Where there is a door between the garage and the house, it must be a solid-core door for fire protection. Most communities require that an automatic door closer be installed on a door in this location.

4. Few codes require that the garage walls be finished inside. However, when the house and garage are attached, the common wall must be finished with plaster or gypsum board, sufficient to retard a fire for one hour if it should start in the garage.

5. If an electric garage door operator is to be installed, an electric outlet will be needed in the ceiling.

6. By placing the garage door as close as 6 in. to the right-side corner of the garage, as in **Fig. 113**, maximum use of this minimum garage space is permitted. When a garage is planned in this way, the drivers of both cars can get out on the left side.

7. A storage shelf can be placed over the hood of a vehicle when there is no other available storage space.

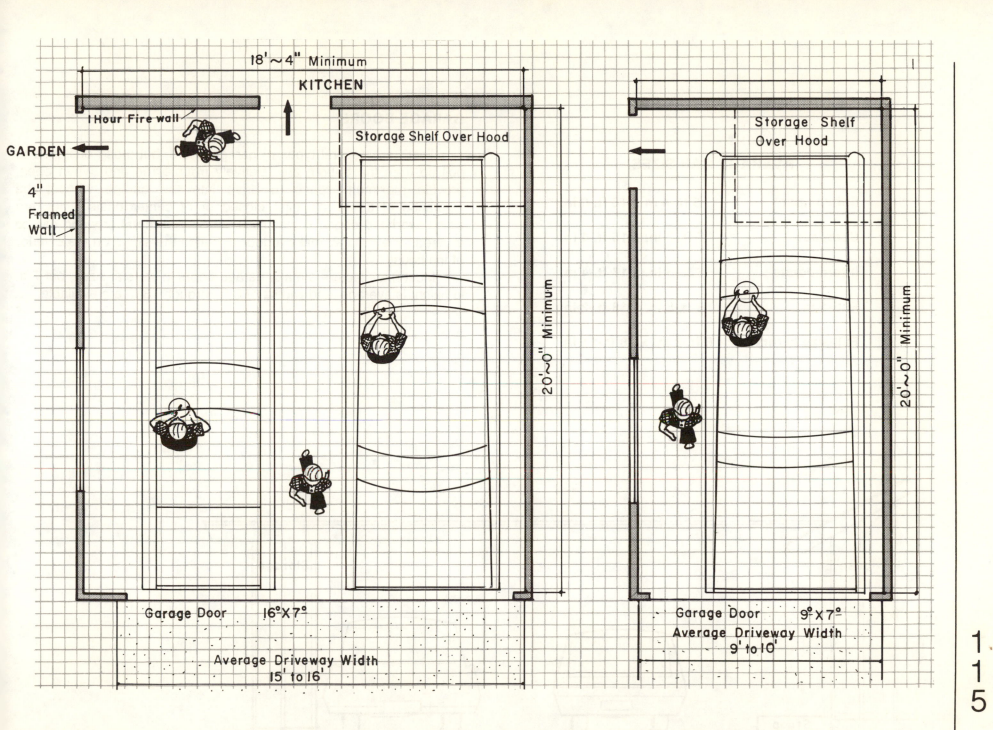

18'~4" Minimum

KITCHEN

1 Hour Fire wall

Storage Shelf Over Hood

GARDEN ←

4"
Framed
Wall

20'~0" Minimum

Garage Door   16°X7°

Average Driveway Width
15' to 16'

Storage Shelf
Over Hood

20'~0" Minimum

Garage Door   9°X7°
Average Driveway Width
9' to 10'

Figure 113.   Minimum-sized, two-car garage and driveway.

Figure 114.   Minimum-sized, one-car garage and driveway.

AVERAGE CAR SIZES

Subcompact	**5 ft.-4 in x 13 ft.-6 in.**
Compact	**5 ft.-7 in. x 15 ft.-4 in.**
Intermediate	**6 ft.-5 in. x 17 ft.-4 in.**
Full-size	**6 ft.-6 in. x 18 ft.-2 in.**
Full-size luxury	**6 ft.-8 in. x 18 ft.-11 in.**

GARAGE DOORS

There are several types of garage doors, but those designed to pull up from the bottom are relatively trouble-free and, when open, provide maximum space to drive into the garage without the hindrance of doors swinging closed or of center posts. They are called **overhead doors**. A manufactured door of **metal** or **wood** can be ordered, or a mill can make a door to match the siding on the exterior of the house.

Most manufacturers make garage doors in several sizes, but 7 ft. in height is average, and widths of 8 ft. through 18 ft. are available.

116

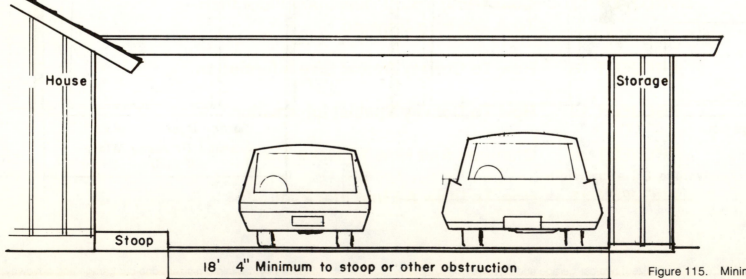

Figure 115.   Minimum width for a two-car carport.

CHAPTER NINE

DEVELOPING THE OVER-ALL PLAN

PROJECT 17   **Converting Your Preliminary Floor Plan To A Working Drawing**

Objective: *To draw a final plan from which the house can be built.*

Materials Required: *A 1/4-in. scale ruler, design guides, all your preliminary drawings, sketches, lists, large sheets of squared drawing paper, tracing paper of equal size, pencils, eraser, colored pencil, drafting tape*

WHAT IS A WORKING DRAWING?

A completed floor plan is referred to as a working drawing because it is the plan used to guide and instruct those who will work on the construction of the house.

The final stage of floor-plan development is the preparation of a working drawing. When you are satisfied with your preliminary plan, you will be ready to prepare the more complete and finalized working drawing.

FROM PRELIMINARY PLAN... TO WORKING DRAWING

1. Secure a large sheet of squared drawing paper to your drawing surface.

2. Referring to your preliminary floor plan and your room studies, lay out the exterior walls of your plan with light pressure on a hard, sharp pencil, in accurate 1/4-in. scale. Start the drawing at the top left-hand corner of the plan at the intersection of two of the heavier blue lines on the paper.

3. If you keep your exterior measurements in even increments of 2 ft. or 4 ft. (as indicated by the heavier blue lines on the paper), the house will be easier to build because framing will be simplified and there will be less material wasted. Many materials are manufactured in sheets that measure 4 ft. x 8 ft.

4. Draw in the interior partitions with a light line, as in drawing the preliminary plan.

5. Carefully measure and draw the kitchen cabinets, sink, and appliances. Refer to **Pages 75-80**.

6. Draw the bathroom fixtures and cabinets. Refer to **Pages 71-74**.

7. Place the windows and write the size of each on the plan in the location selected. Refer to window information given on **Pages 68-70**.

8. After reviewing the furniture arrangement in your preliminary studies, draw in the doors, indicating the size of each and the direction of swing or slide. See **Pages 64-65**.

9. Referring to **Pages 66** and **67**, draw in the wardrobe doors and indicate the size of each.

10. Referring to the furniture arrangement in your preliminary studies and the direction of the door swings on your working drawing, draw the electrical outlets, switches, and lights. This can best be done by fastening a piece of tracing paper large enough to cover the entire plan over your work. When you have carefully planned the switches and outlets on the tracing paper, transfer the symbols to the working drawing. Refer to **Figs. 97-99** and **Fig. 112**.

11. Print or write the name of each room and of any important items on the plan. Refer to **Fig. 116** and **Project 19**, **Page 123**.

12. When most of the details have been drawn on the plan, go over the wall lines with a heavier pressure on your pencil. A softer lead is desirable for this job. See **Page 22** for recommended lead choices.

13. When all the walls are clearly and sharply defined, the drawing will be much easier to work with. This is a good time to re-evaluate what you have drawn. Study the details carefully and compare them with your preliminary and plot-plan studies.

14. Dimension your drawing and add any necessary notes. Refer to **Fig. 117** on **Page 121** and to **Projects 18** and **19** for simplified methods of dimensioning and making notes.

15. Double-check your drawing to see that you have included all necessary details by comparing it with **Fig. 117**.

16. Shade the walls with a colored pencil. If you remove your drawing from the drawing surface and shade the walls on the back of the paper, it will be easier to erase wall lines when making changes.

17. The plumbing, electrical, and mechanical details of the plan should be drawn after consulting with contractors in the respective fields (called subcontractors), particularly if you have no prior experience in drawing plans.

18. This is an excellent time to have several prints made from it. See **Chapter 15** for information about blueprinting and whiteprinting.

19. A print of the plan can be given to each of the subcontractors consulted, to take and study. Each subcontractor will usually sketch his/her segment of the work on an individual print.

20. Each subcontractor, such as electrical, plumbing, heating and cooling, etc., is knowledgable in planning his/her segment of the work according to the local building codes. The prints on which subcontractors have worked out details should be stapled together with prints of your other drawings, and submitted to the building department when applying for building permits.

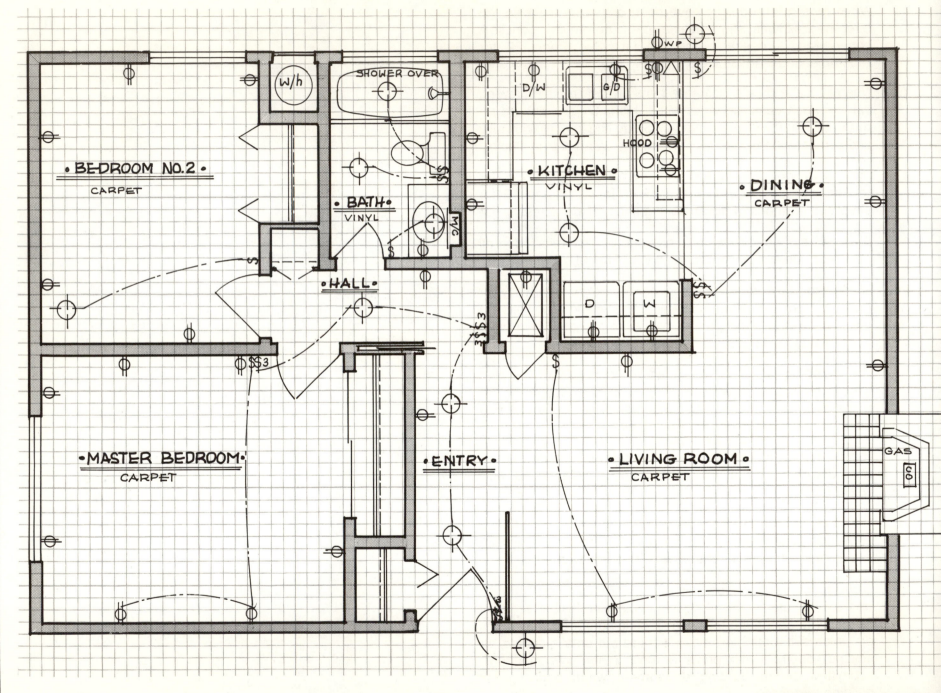

Figure 116.   A working drawing.

120

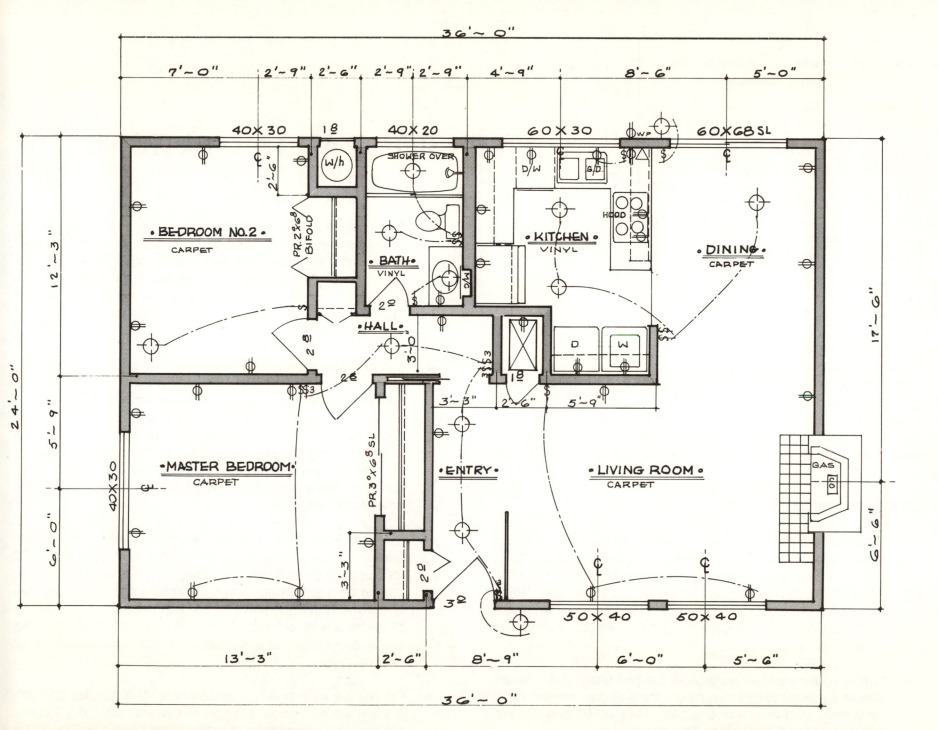

Figure 117.   A working drawing with dimensions added.

121

DIMENSIONS AND NOTATIONS

WHAT ARE DIMENSIONS?

Dimensions are figures which indicate *actual* sizes on scale drawings. Each person involved in the construction of the house will expect to find the information needed to do his/her part of the work on the prints. Consequently, the drawings must clearly show over-all measurements of the house, specific measurements of the interior spaces, and all details.

DRAWING DIMENSION LINES:

1. Lines drawn for the purpose of showing where a measurement begins and ends are called dimension lines. They are placed, in most cases, around the exterior perimeter of the floor plan. Many of the dimensions can be shown on these lines. Room and hall measurements are placed within the plan where necessary for clarity. **Figure 117** is an example of simplified *dimensioning*.

2. **The first dimension line** around the perimeter of the house should be about 3/4 in. away from the wall line, leaving room for writing window and door sizes; 1/4 to 1/2 in. between the first and **second dimension line** is sufficient.

3. **Extension lines** are lines which extend from all exterior corners of the building. See **Fig. 117**. They serve the purpose of showing the beginning and ending of a dimension line. A mark is placed where dimension lines intersect with extension lines. Some drafters make this mark with arrows, others use dots or slashes (called hash marks). Use the mark you prefer.

4. **A centerline** designates the center of a given area. The word centerline if often abbreviated as **CL**. To designate a centerline on the plan, a line is drawn through the center of any given space with a short dash at each end and the centerline symbol. See **Fig. 117**. In *dimensioning*, a centerline is usually placed along perimeter dimension lines, extending through the exact center of each window and each interior partition. When used in this way it serves the same purpose as an extension line.

5. When drawing dimension and extension lines, use a light pressure on a well-pointed, fairly hard lead. See **Page 22** for suggested lead choices. They are the lightest lines to appear on the drawing. When dimension and extension lines are drawn correctly, they will not be confused with the lines of the structure, but will be dark enough to reproduce when prints are made. See **Chapter 15** for information about printing plans.

6. Figures are written in feet and inches; for example, 10′ - 6″. If there are no inches, the figure is written 10′ - 0″. Figures are always written above the dimension lines; see **Fig. 117**.

ADDING NOTATIONS TO YOUR DRAWING:

1. **Special notations** are frequently necessary on the plan. There is not much room for these notes by the time all of the other information has been drawn or written on the plan. They should be added in small legible writing or printing. Place them as close to the object they describe as possible. Use a small curved arrow to connect the note to the object it denotes. When there are too many notes, information can be written on separate sheets of paper. Pages of information relating to the plan are called *specifications*.

2. **The name of each room** is written on the plan. Bedrooms are identified as "MASTER BEDROOM," "BEDROOM NO. 2," "BEDROOM NO. 3," etc. Or they could be identified as owner's bedroom, girl's bedroom, boy's bedroom, etc.

3. **The scale** in which the plan has been drawn is always indicated at the bottom of the sheet in the following way: SCALE: 1/4″ = 1′-0″.

4. **The name of the owner** of the property and the address of the property are always included at the bottom right-hand corner of the page. The name and telephone number of the person preparing the plans should be included with this information.

5. **Number each page** of the set of plans: "No. 1 - PLOT PLAN," "No. 2 - FLOOR PLAN," No. 3 - ELEVATIONS," etc.

6. **The total square footage** of the house, plus that of the garage should be placed at the bottom of the sheet.

Objective: *To learn how to handle suggestions for changes in the plan made by subcontractors and others and to make them on the drawings.*

Materials Required: *A 1/4-in. scale ruler, design guides, your floor plan, tracing paper, pencils, eraser, colored pencil*

EVALUATE SUBCONTRACTORS' SUGGESTIONS

1. When each subcontractor returns the print with suggestions, you can begin to finalize the plan.

2. Space requirements for such things as heating and cooling units and ducts (chambers through which the cooled or heated air flows), plumbing pipes in the walls, and the electric panel may necessitate some changes in the plan.

3. Each person working with the plan will make suggestions for changes. It is well to keep an open mind in regard to changes at this point. Try to visualize the changes suggested by others. Some will be necessary if specific equipment is to be used, others will not. Sometimes changes can be avoided by using another kind of equipment, appliance, or fixture.

4. If, *after evaluating each suggestion*, you decide not to make the change, stay with your decision. Do not let a hodgepodge of suggestions destroy the integrity of your plan. Only you know what your real goal is. You must make the final decisions after carefully evaluating all the facts available to you.

5. Most changes can be made on the plan by erasing carefully. Drafting papers are made strong enough to withstand repeated erasures; however, if the drawing is becoming smeared and untidy, and there are a great many changes to be made, it would be advisable to fasten a fresh piece of squared drawing paper over the original drawing and match up the squares. Trace the accurate parts of the drawing and make the changes as you work. Save time by testing changes first on tracing paper overlays.

NOTE: Keep in mind that it is much easier to change and redraw your plans than it is to knock out walls and make changes during the course of construction - and certainly less costly.

6. One of the most frequent causes of costly mistakes on drawings is changes. When one thing is changed, it often affects something else. When your plans have progressed to an advanced stage before changes are made, be sure to check everything you have drawn against your original studies to make certain you have made all relevant changes and to study the effect the change will have on the total plan. For example, moving a door or changing the direction it swings could necessitate relocation of a light switch.

PLANNING FOR LATER ADDITIONS

If the plan is to add items or space to the house at a later time, it is best not to include them on the working drawing, but rather to keep them on a separate copy for your own future reference. The only exception to this would be instances where some work is to be done during construction in order to make later additions possible; for example, pipes in the walls (rough plumbing) for a future bathroom or electrical wiring for an appliance to be added later.

COMPLETE YOUR PLOT PLAN

PROJECT 21   **How To Draw A Final Plot Plan**

Objective: *To draw a plan of the lot showing the placement of the house and enough other information to acquaint workers with the project requirements.*

Materials Required: *The 1/16-in. scale ruler from Page 229, a small sheet of squared drawing paper, your original plot plan drawing, sketches and notes, tracing paper, pencil, eraser, colored pencil, drafting tape*

1. Referring to your original plot plan studies, lay out and draw the lot on a fresh sheet of squared drawing paper.

2. Draw in a scale of 1/16 in. = 1 ft.

3. Refer to **Fig. 32** on **Page 49** for plot-plan symbols and designations.

4. Locate and indicate any trees, buildings, fences, or other **existing features** that are to remain on the lot.

5. Mark them "existing."

6. Draw the house and vehicle shelter in the chosen location. If you have not verified the setback requirements with your local planning department, this is the time to do so.

7. Draw all areas that are to be concrete, such as the driveway, walkways, terraces or patios, porches, etc. These areas should be dimensioned and the designation for concrete used. See **Figs. 113** and **114**, **Page 115** for driveway requirements. During construction, the concrete is usually placed according to the information given on the plot plan.

8. Indicate on the plot plan the proposed location for a well and/or septic system and leaching lines (part of the septic system) if required. Information about this can be obtained from your local department of health and sanitation. If city facilities are available, indicate the place where water and sewer lines will come onto the property.

9. If natural gas is available, show the location of the line coming onto the property. If other fuel is to be used, such as butane, propane, or oil, show the location of the storage tank.

10. Check with the electric company for the location of the power source which will serve the proposed home. The closest existing source (pole) is not necessarily the one that will be used to serve the property. Indicate the location of the power source.

11. Double-check your drawing with **Fig. 118.**

12. Go over the lines of the drawing with a heavier pressure on your well-pointed lead.

13. Add the **arrow** indicating "north," the **address** or **legal description** of the property, the **name** of the owner, and the **scale** in which the plan is drawn. This information can be placed at the bottom of the page.

14. A separate print of your plot plan can also be used for planning your landscaping.

15. Subcontractors may also need a copy of your completed plot plan. All information should be confirmed at this time.

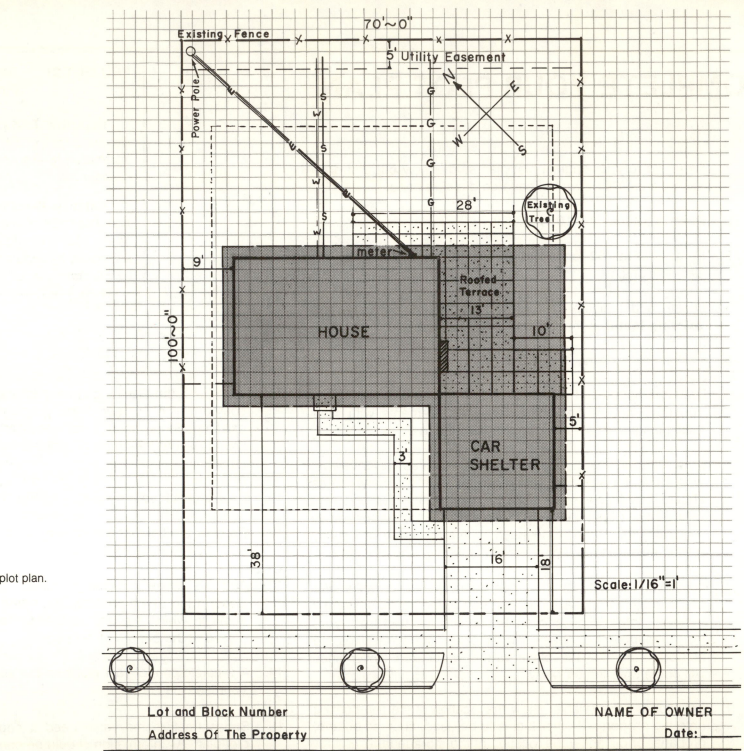

Figure 118.   A completed plot plan.

CHAPTER TEN

REVISING EXISTING PLANS

PROJECT 22   **How To Analyze The Plan And Draw The Changes**

THE ART OF REVISING PLANS

The growing popularity of house plan services has created a demand for information about revising existing or purchased plans.

A plan is often found attractive because of one or two outstanding features that seem particularly suited for the new home. However, careful analysis usually reveals several things that should be revised.

If revisions are made carefully, with skill and thought, the results can be quite satisfactory - even outstanding! If the project is to revise a floor plan, the information, scale rulers, and design guides in this book will help you to make the necessary changes or additions so that the revised plan loses nothing of its original attractiveness, meets requirements, and may be oriented to advantage on the lot.

NOTE: The objective of an individual revising a plan should be to retain all of its attractive and functional features, while incorporating the desired changes.

ELEMENTS OF GOOD DESIGN

When a floor plan has been skillfully drawn, all the component parts fit together like a jigsaw puzzle:

1. All spaces are correct in size for the use to which they will be put and are conveniently oriented to each other.

2. Bathroom and kitchen locations have been analyzed in relation to plumbing problems.

3. Cabinets and storage facilities are conveniently arranged and in keeping with the size of the house.

4. Traffic patterns throughout the house have been given careful consideration.

5. Mechanical equipment, such as heating and cooling, is properly located and sized according to requirements.

6. Lighting and other electrical facilities are located for maximum convenience.

7. The exterior design has been carefully coordinated with the interior design.

8. The roof style and shape are related to the shape of the floor plan and the overall design concept.

FIRST BEGIN WITH A SUITABLE FLOOR PLAN

Not all floor plans lend themselves well to changes and additions. The plan selected should require the very minimum number of alterations.

Any plan selected should be studied for suitability of design. The size of the house, as well as the size of the individual rooms, is an important consideration, as this influences its ultimate cost.

Another factor that should not be overlooked is the suitability of the plan for the building site and local weather conditions.

PUT YOUR PLAN TO THE TEST

The only way you can really be sure that the right plan has been selected for the purpose is to subject it to the following tests:

1. Make a small-scale drawing of the lot by following the instructions given in **Project 7** "Drawing a Plot Plan," **Page 44**. Also review **Project 6**, "Learning to Think in 1/8-in. and 1/16-in. scale," **Page 40**.

2. Make the first study of the plan by sketching it on your plot plan, as in **Project 11**, "Sketching a Planning Diagram," **Page 94**. Fasten tracing paper over your plot-plan drawing and make several quick, sketchy diagrams of the house and car shelter on the tracing paper, like those in **Fig. 100**, **Page 95**.

3. Study the best use of the lot space as explained in **Project 9**, "Fitting the House to the Lot," **Figures 39 - 42** on **Pages 58-61** show examples of a house and car shelter arranged on a lot in four different ways.

PROJECT 22   How To Analyze The Plan And Draw The Changes

Objective: *To learn how to analyze an existing floor plan - mail order or other - and revise, modify, or add to it.*

Materials Required: *The 1/4-in. scale ruler from Page 229, design guides from Pages 215-227, squared drawing paper, the plan to be revised, all available information about the lot, lists of requirements, sizes of furniture, equipment, etc. to be used in the new home, larger sheets of squared drawing paper, tracing paper of equal size, pencils, erasers, colored pencil, drafting tape*

---

4. Reverse the plan if necessary or desirable. If, as you try different planning arrangements on tracing paper laid over your plot plan, you find that there are problems such as a poorly located driveway, the sun striking the house on the wrong side, or bedrooms on the noisy side of the lot, try turning over your planning diagram (which has been drawn on translucent paper), thereby reversing the plan. Lay the reversed plan on the plot plan for study. This will show you how a reversed version of the plan will work on the lot. This simple trick often makes considerable difference in the livability of a home. Refer to **Figs. 123** and **124** on **Page 136**.

5. If you are looking at a photographically reduced version of the plan, it will not be easy to judge the size of the house. You will need to redraw the plan to the scale of 1/4 in. = 1 ft., in order to determine the total square footage and to verify that it meets your space requirements. A review of **Project 2**, "Thinking in Scale," on **Page 26**, and **Project 4**, "How to Measure and Draw a Room from a Plan," on **Page 30**, will refresh your memory on working in 1/4-in. scale.

HOW TO REVISE THE PLAN

DRAWING THE INTERIOR:

1. **Projects 12**, "Preparing to Sketch a Preliminary Floor Plan," **Page 97**, and **Project 13**, "Sketching a Preliminary Floor Plan," **Pages 98-99**, will instruct you in the procedure for drawing a plan in 1/4-in. scale. This is to be done on a larger sheet of squared drawing paper. If there are no dimensions (measurements) on the plan you have, and it has been photographically reduced so that you cannot scale it, you can use the length of the bathtub (almost always 5 ft.) or the depth of the kitchen base cabinets (always 2 ft.) as your guide.

2. When the plan is redrawn in a scale of 1/4 in. = 1 ft., you will be sure of the exterior dimensions and can calculate the square footage in the plan accurately. This is easy to do, and the procedure is explained fully in **Project 14**, "Figuring Square Footage," on **Page 99**.

3. It is important that you carefully study each of the rooms in the plan to be sure that they meet requirements and will accommodate the furnishings. Work out the details for each room in the plan by following the step-by-step procedure depicted in **Figures 103 - 112**, **Project 15**, "How to Draw Room Studies," starting on **Page 102**.

When you have completed the necessary studies of the plan and are sure that the best possible plan for the purpose has been selected, you will be ready to make the required changes.

FLOOR-PLAN EXAMPLES

Figs. **119** and **121** are floor-plan examples. Various changes have been made on these plans in Figs. **120** and **122**. Note that the changes are very simple and have been made without changing the exterior design radically.

ROOF CHANGES

Where additions have been made, note that difficult roof changes have been avoided.

MOVING PARTITIONS

The current practice of constructing a roof with prefabricated trusses (**Fig. 133**, **Page 157**) make it possible, in designing a small home, to place interior partitions wherever they are desirable. When roof trusses are used, the outside walls of the house are the bearing walls and carry the weight of the roof (called the roof load). Therefore, you can relocate or remove partitions in accordance with your plan revisions, assuming that you are revising an uncomplicated plan for a relatively small home.

ADDING PLUMBING

If extra bathroom facilities are planned, it is often economical to keep areas requiring plumbing as close together as possible. It would be advisable to consult a plumber about the feasibility of your ideas, if you plan substantial plumbing changes. Plumbing is one area of construction where cost is often related to the location of fixtures.

MAKING THE DESIRED CHANGES:

1. Fasten your preliminary 1/4-in. scale drawing of the original plan onto your drawing board.

2. Cover it with an overlay of tracing paper securely fastened to the board.

3. Sketch in the desired changes on the tracing paper.

4. Make as many of these sketches as necessary to get the changes exactly as you want them. Consider all aspects carefully and evaluate each change and its effect on the over-all plan.

5. Select your final and best sketch and draw a more carefully prepared preliminary drawing, as shown in **Project 13**, "Sketching a Preliminary Floor Plan," **Page 98**.

6. When you are satisfied that your preliminary floor plan reflects the required changes, proceed to **Project 17**, "Converting Your Preliminary Floor Plan to a Working Drawing," **Page 118** and draw the plan in more careful detail.

DRAWING THE EXTERIOR:

1. If you have 1/4-in scale drawings of the exterior of the house, (called elevations) trace them on a large sheet of squared drawing paper.

2. Any changes or additions that have been made to the plan can be handled as in **Project 28**, "Drawing the Exterior of the House," **Page 151**.

3. Also see **Fig. 129**, **Page 152**. (Exception: Weights of lines used to depict the original part of the plan in **Fig. 129** would be the same as those used to depict the revised portions of the drawing.)

4. If exterior drawings for the plan are not available to you, you can plan and draw them by following the simplified, step-by-step system given in **Chapter 14**, "Drawing Plans For the Exterior of a House."

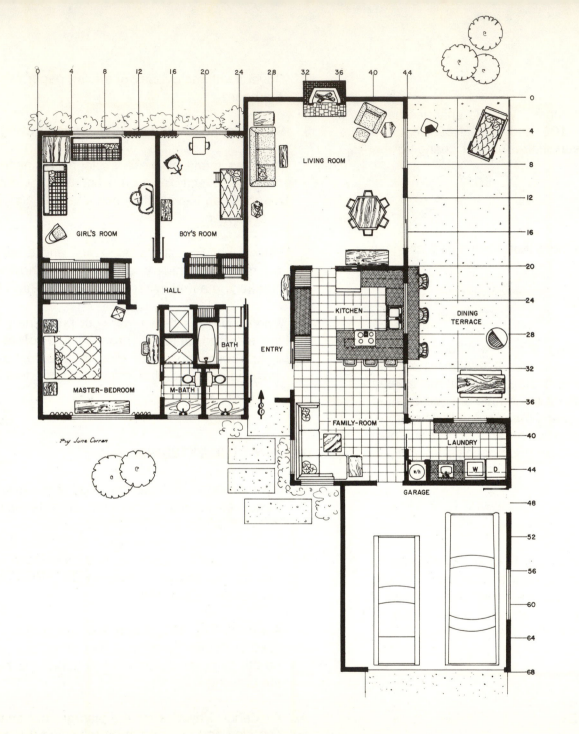

Figure 119.   Floor plan No. 1.

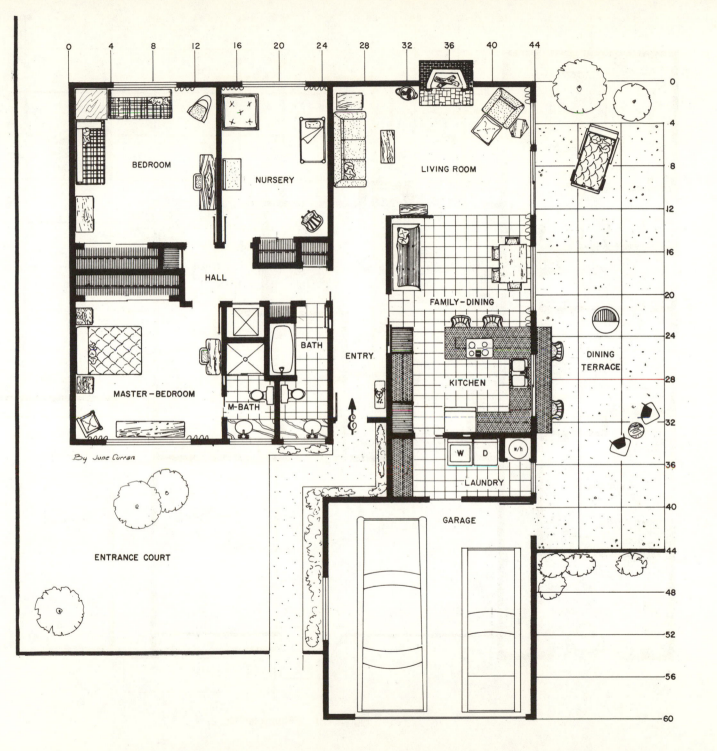

BEDROOM

NURSERY

LIVING ROOM

HALL

FAMILY—DINING

MASTER—BEDROOM

BATH

ENTRY

KITCHEN

DINING
TERRACE

M-BATH

LAUNDRY

By June Curran

W D w/h

GARAGE

ENTRANCE COURT

1
3
3

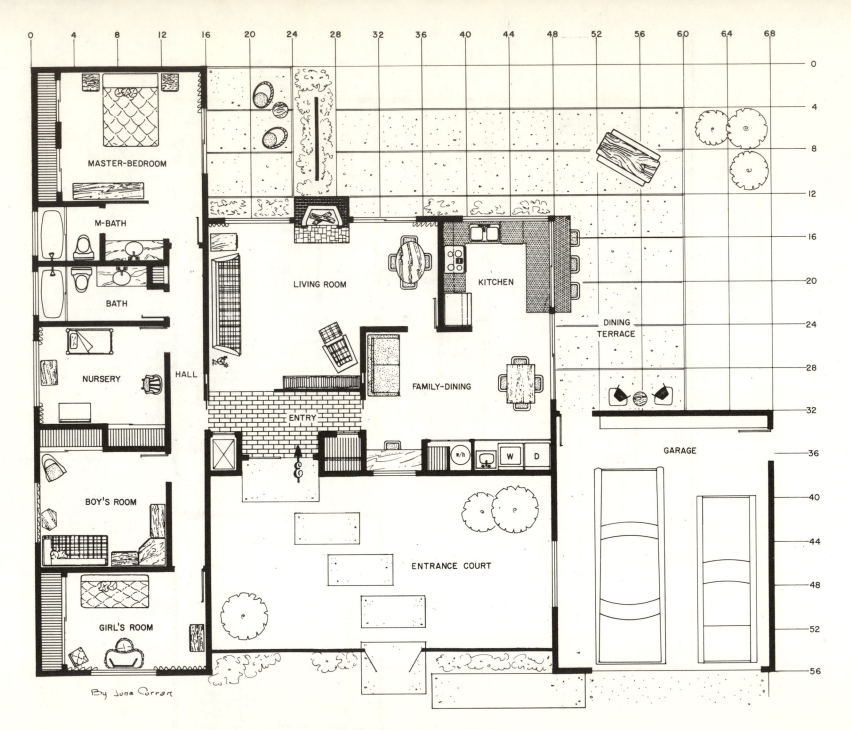

By June Curran

Figure 121. Floor plan No. 2.

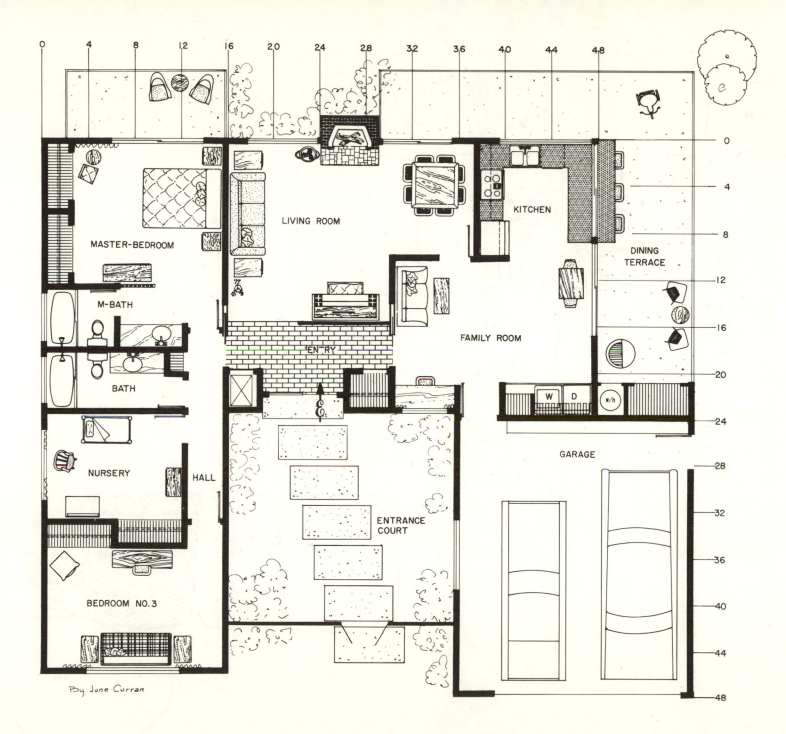

Figure 122.   Floor plan No. 2, revised.

135

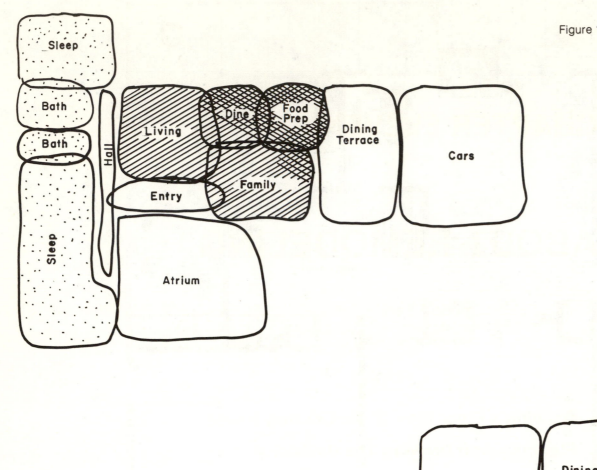

Figure 123.   A planning diagram from an existing floor plan.

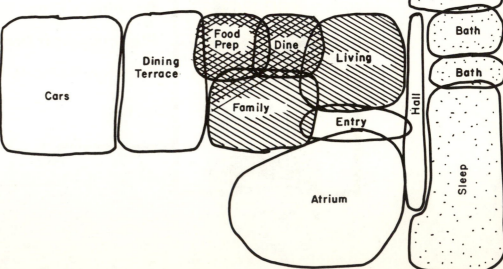

Figure 124.   A reverse plan from the same existing floor plan.

CHAPTER ELEVEN

MORE ABOUT REMODELING

BEGIN WITH A PLAN OF THE EXISTING HOUSE

When one is planning a remodeling project, it is essential to begin with a complete plan of the existing house.

After you have drawn in 1/4-in. scale, it will be much easier for everyone involved in the project to visualize the desired revisions. When you are working on paper, solutions to space arrangement problems will occur to you that might not otherwise be evident.

MEASURING THE HOUSE

In order to draw an accurate plan of the house, you will need measurements. The first measurements to be taken are of the exterior walls of the house. These are to be *horizontal* measurements.

HOW TO MEASURE THE EXTERIOR OF THE HOUSE:

1. Fasten a piece of letter-sized scratch paper to a clipboard or other firm, portable working surface.

2. Walk around the outside of the house and make a rough sketch of the exterior shape, noting the jogs and offsets. Disregard the windows and doors.

3. Using the longest tape measure you can obtain, measure the exterior of the house and note the measurements on the sketch. When you are measuring, have someone hold the other end of the tape measure and place it on the wall above plants and shrubs.

4. Correct the jogs and offsets as necessary on your sketch, and write in the measurements accurately.

5. Measure the thickness of the exterior wall as revealed in a window or a doorway. Do not include casing or molding thickness.

HOW TO MEASURE THE INTERIOR OF THE HOUSE:

The procedure for measuring and drawing an individual room in a home is given in **Project 5**, "How to Measure and Draw an Actual Room," **Page 34**.

1. On individual pieces of scratch paper clipped to a board, make sketches of the interior of each room as shown in **Fig. 20**, **Page 35**. Identify each room by name. Measure a corner room first.

2. Measure the thickness of the interior partitions in the house. You will probably find that they are all the same thickness unless there is special treatment on one of the walls, such as brick or paneling.

DRAWING A FLOOR PLAN OF THE EXISTING HOUSE

HOW TO DRAW THE EXTERIOR WALLS:

1. Securely fasten a large piece of translucent squared drawing paper to your working surface.

2. Lay out and draw lines to represent the *perimeter* of the exterior wall, using light pressure on your well-sharpened pencil. Start the drawing with the upper left corner of the plan at the intersection of two of the heavier blue lines on the squared paper.

3. Draw a second line *inside* the first, completely *around the perimeter* of the house plan. This line represents the *inside* of the perimeter wall. In most cases, the wall thickness will be 6 in., represented by one square on the paper. Use your scale ruler when measuring and drawing walls of other thicknesses.

4. If the house has two or more stories, you will need a plan of each floor to be remodeled. Use a separate sheet of squared drawing paper for each floor. When drawings are complete, one plan can be placed over the other to check for accuracy of alignment.

HOW TO DRAW THE INTERIOR OF THE HOUSE:

1. With all your sketches in order for convenient reference, proceed to draw in the interior partitions, using the 1/4-in. scale ruler where necessary. Make notations of room measurements on your plan, or keep your dimensioned sketches in good order.

2. Tracing from the design guides or using a general purpose template, designate kitchen and bathroom appliances, fixtures, and cabinets on the plan.

3. Designate window and door openings as shown in **Figures 15 and 16**. Note the size of each.

4. Designate the direction in which the doors swing in each room.

5. It would be a convenience to have the electric outlets and switches noted on the plan, especially in areas where revisions are to be made. If you wish to include them, refer to **Page 91** and to **Fig. 99**.

6. When most of the details have been drawn on the plan, go over the wall lines, using a heavier pressure on your pencil. A softer lead is desirable for this job. See **Page 22** for recommended lead choices. All other lines should be heavy enough to be visible through an overlay sheet of squared drawing paper.

STARTING THE

REMODELING PROJECT

When the drawing of the existing house is complete, it will be much easier to plan, visualize, and draw the desired revisions.

HOW TO DRAW REVISIONS ON THE PLAN:

1. Study your completed drawing carefully and make a list of the desired revisions.

2. Tape tracing paper over your floor plan of the existing house and sketch the revisions on the tracing paper.

3. Check to see that your sketches are in scale.

4. Test your revision ideas by placing appliances, fixtures, and furnishings in the new areas and rearranging them in the old. Use design guide cutouts or tracings to facilitate visualization.

5. Verify visually that the new space arrangements you have created on paper are workable by comparing them to similar-sized areas in the home.

6. Take time with this planning and use as many overlay sheets as necessary. Try different possibilities on paper.

Careful planning at this stage of the project will result in the best possible use of the space available. A good plan can save time and money by preventing needless changes and mistakes.

DEVELOPING THE DRAWING:

1. When you are satisfied with your sketch for the proposed changes, remove the tracing paper and cover your original drawing with a fresh piece of squared drawing paper.

2. Trace over the original wall lines of the existing house with a very light pressure on your well-pointed pencil.

3. Refer to your sketched changes and lightly mark, for your own reference, any walls that are to be removed.

4. Walls that are to be removed should be dashed on the plan with a heavier pressure on your well-pointed lead. The designation for walls to be removed is shown in **Fig. 125**. See **Fig. 126** for an example of this designation on a floor plan.

5. Draw in any new walls using a light pressure on your well-pointed lead.

6. Lightly trace the details of cabinetry, fixtures, and appliances that are to remain in the remodeled house.

DESIGNATING NEW WORK:

1. With heavier lines, although not as heavy as wall lines, draw in any cabinetry, fixtures, and appliances that are to be new. Place them in accordance with your new planning sketch. **Chapter 5** gives symbols and designations for designating new work.

2. Designate any door openings or windows that are to be new. Refer to **Fig. 126**.

3. Trace the windows and doors that will remain unchanged in the existing house.

4. Go over all the wall lines, old and new, except those to be removed, with a heavier pressure on your pencil, preferably with a softer lead.

5. Shade the walls that are to be new with a colored pencil. Refer to **Fig. 125.**

Do not shade lines for existing walls which are *not* to be removed.

Use dashed lines where the wall *is* to be removed.

Indicate new walls to be constructed of wood by shading lightly with a colored pencil.

Indicate walls to be constructed of masonry with hashmarks.

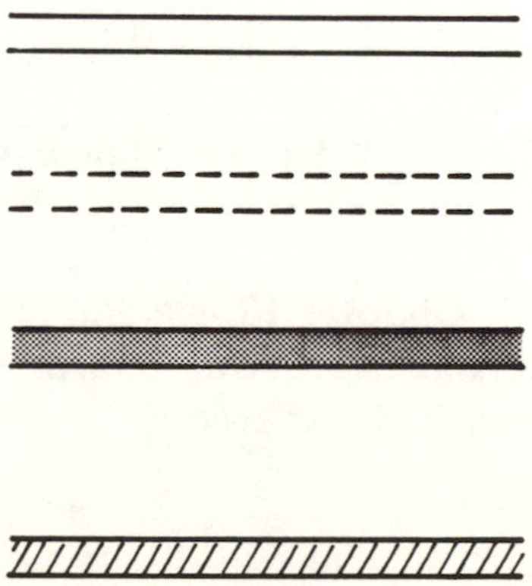

Figure 125. Wall shading.

PROJECT 25	**Drawing Remodeling Plans For The Exterior**

Objective: *To measure the house vertically and prepare drawings of the exterior of the house.*

Materials Required: *To measure: the longest tape measure available, a ladder, scratch paper and clipboard or scratch pad, and a helper. For drawing: A 1/4-in. scale ruler, your sketches and measurements, larger sheets of squared drawing paper, tracing paper of equal size, pencil, eraser, drafting tape*

DRAWING AN EXTERIOR PLAN FOR A REMODELING PROJECT

In many cases, interior remodeling does not affect the exterior. Sometimes a fresh coat of paint is all that is required. If this is true of the remodeling job you are planning, you will not need plans of the exterior. However, interior remodeling may create a need for new windows and changed door locations. In some cases, complete modernization of the exterior is desirable.

When alterations are to be made to the exterior, it is advisable to make drawings that show clearly the work to be done. Your project will become much more clear and understandable to everyone involved when you have drawings that show the exterior of the house as it will be when the changes are made. **Chapter 14** explains the procedure to follow for making exterior drawings. Remodeling drawings for exteriors are made in the same way as drawings for a new home; however, you will need some measurements.

MEASURING THE EXTERIOR VERTICALLY:

1. The measurements taken for drawing the floor plan gave you the horizontal dimensions (along the ground line).

2. In order to draw exterior views of the home, (called elevations), you will need vertical measurements (from the ground to the top of the roof) of the existing house. **Figures 127 and 127a** show the points of measurements to be taken.

3. Make a sketch of each side of the house and write in the necessary measurements.

4. The widths of windows and doors do not have to be measured again. The information can be taken from the floor plan. Measure the height of each as shown in **Figs. 127 and 127a**.

DRAWING ELEVATIONS (EXTERIOR DRAWINGS) OF THE EXISTING HOUSE:

1. Refer to **Project 30**, "Drawing Elevations," **Page 162**, for information about drawing the exterior plan of the existing house.

2. Following the steps outlined in **Chapter 14**, but substituting measurements of the existing house, draw elevation views of each side of the house.

3. See **Fig. 149**, **Page 178**, for information on drawing roof designs.

SKETCHING THE CHANGES:

1. When your drawing of the exterior of the house is complete, you can fasten tracing paper over it in preparation for drawing the revisions.

2. Make as many quick sketches as possible on tracing paper overlays in order to achieve the best possible solution to design problems.

3. In designing the exterior, avoid a mixture of styles and treatments. Try for continuity of design. In *restoration projects,* it is important to retain original design concepts.

DRAWING THE NEW WORK:

1. Redraw the elevations, showing the new work to be done. This is done by using different weights of lines to differentiate the existing house from the new work. Refer to **Fig. 129**.

2. Write "New Work" in the areas of change.

3. Dimension all new work clearly.

Chapter 13, starting on **Page 155**, gives other information about construction terms and procedures that will be useful to you when making this drawing.

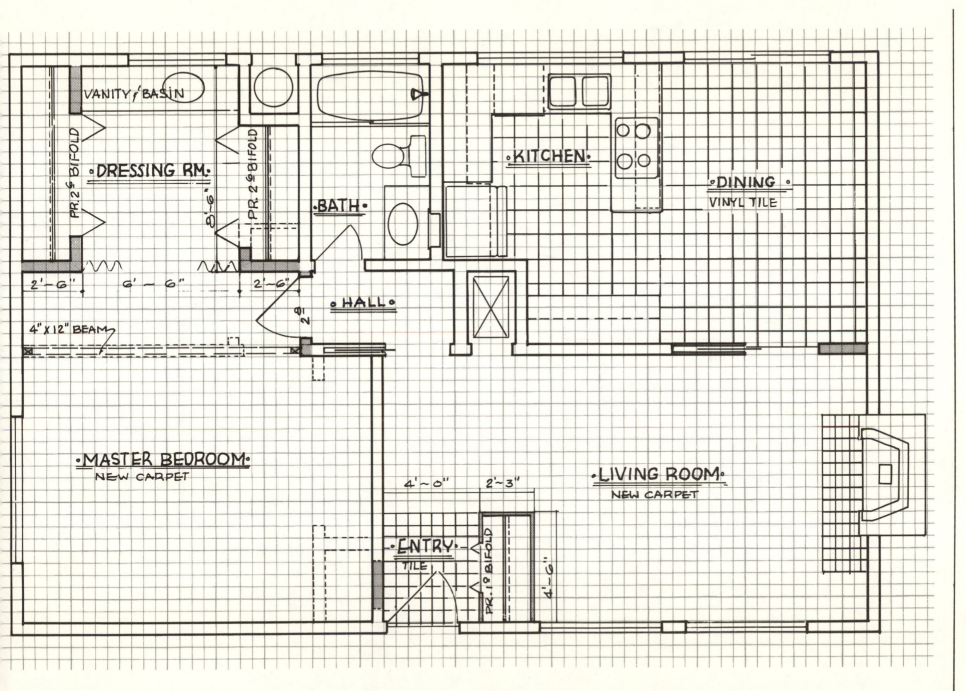

VANITY & BASIN

PR. 2⁹ BIFOLD

DRESSING RM.

PR. 2⁹ BIFOLD

6'-6"

BATH .

KITCHEN .

. DINING .
VINYL TILE

2'-6"   6'-6"   2'-6"

. HALL .

4"×12" BEAM

2'8"

. MASTER BEDROOM .
NEW CARPET

. LIVING ROOM .
NEW CARPET

4'-0"   2'-3"

. ENTRY .
TILE

PR. 1⁹ BIFOLD

4'-6"

143

Figure 126.   A floor plan for a home to be remodeled. (Refer to the original plan, Fig. 13.)

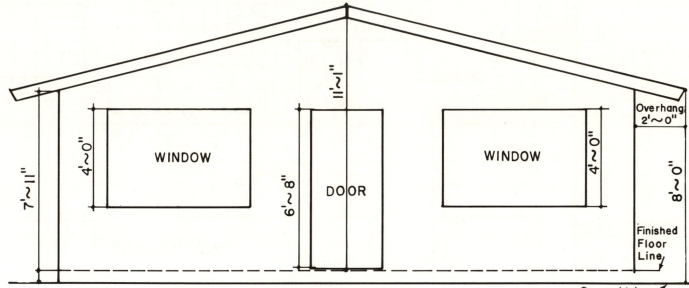

Figure 127.   Measuring a one-story house.

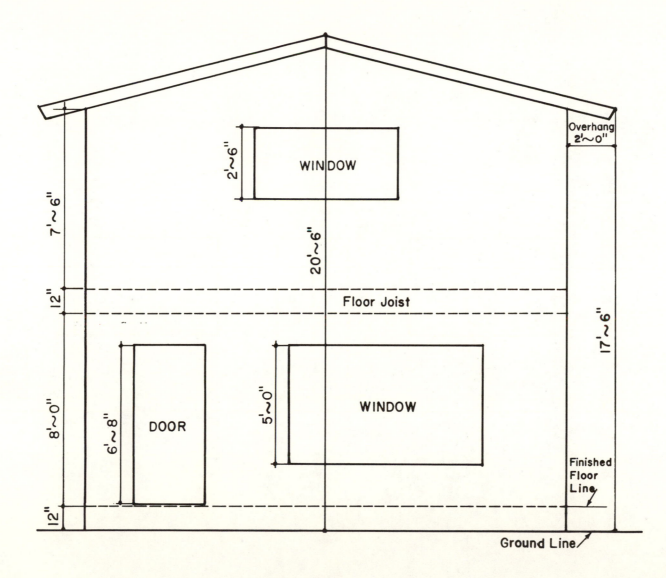

Figure 127a.   Measuring a two-story house.

CHAPTER TWELVE

MORE ABOUT PLANNING
AN ADDITION

Objective: *To make a floor-plan-type drawing of the house showing exterior measurements and shape in 1/4-in. scale. Also to draw a plot plan of the lot, showing placement of the house, thus revealing the space available for the addition.*

Materials Required: *A 1/4-in. scale ruler, larger sheets of squared drawing paper, pencil, eraser, colored pencil, drafting tape*

OVER-ALL PLANNING OF HOUSE, LOT, AND ADDITION

The procedure for drawing plans for an addition is similar to that of drawing plans for remodeling. However, when you plan to make an addition to a home, you must make an over-all plan. Take into consideration the size and shape of the house, the lot, existing car facilities, space available for the addition, local building regulations, etc.

THE IMPORTANCE OF A PLOT PLAN

The best way to visualize an addition to a home is on a plot plan, where you can clearly see the relationship of the addition to the existing house and to the lot. When the existing house is drawn on a plot plan you can also study the orientation of the house and the proposed addition to the sun and to the neighbors properties.

Complete information is given about drawing plot plans in **Project 7**, "Drawing a Plot Plan," **Page 44**. You will also find helpful information in **Project 9**, "Fitting the House to the Lot," **Page 57**.

HOW TO DRAW THE EXISTING HOUSE ON A PLOT PLAN:

1. Draw a plot plan of the lot on a piece of squared paper secured to your drawing surface. Use a light pressure on your well-sharpened pencil.

2. Draw the existing house and all other features on your plot plan. Include the car shelter, paved areas, driveway, trees, and garden areas.

3. Go over all the lines with heavier pressure on your pencil when the plot plan has been completed as shown in **Fig. 118.**

4. Add accurate size information. For dimensioning procedures, see **Project 18**, "How to Convey Actual Size Information," **Page 122**.

5. Sketch in the addition on a piece of tracing paper fastened over your completed plot plan.

6. Try several different shapes and space arrangements and experiment with all possibilities. Make as many overlays as necessary to achieve an addition that seems to satisfy your needs and fit within the setback requirements.

NOTE: If you are not sure what the setback requirements are on the lot you are working with, this would be a good time to check with someone in your local planning or building department. You can then make accurate plans.

DRAWING A FLOOR PLAN OF THE EXISTING HOUSE

If the plan is to add on to one part of the house and make no further changes, it may not be necessary to draw a floor plan of the existing house; but a floor plan of the house as well as the addition will help you to visualize the space relationship between the existing and the new areas. New ways to effectively rearrange space and furniture within the existing house may also become evident. Information on drawing a floor plan of an existing house is given in **Project 23**, "Drawing a Floor Plan of An Existing House." **Figure 128** shows a partial plan of an existing house with a new addition.

When you have drawn the necessary floor plan of the existing house and completed the plot plan, you will be ready to make plans for the addition.

HOW TO DRAW PLANS FOR THE ADDITION:

1. Sketch the addition according to your planning on tracing paper fastened securely over the floor plan of the existing house.

2. Make an overlay of the original drawing, using a fresh piece of squared drawing paper, and trace the wall lines of the existing house with a light pressure on your well-sharpened pencil.

3. Use dashed lines to represent walls to be removed.

4. Add the lines representing the walls of the addition. Designate any new windows and doors. Lines representing new walls are to be shaded according to the legend in **Fig. 125**.

5. Draw any remaining details, such as kitchen and bathroom fixtures, cabinetry, and wiring diagram. Refer to **Chapter 5** for symbols and designations, starting on **Page 63**.

PROJECT 27   Drawing The Addition

Objective: *To draw a plan for an addition that will serve your needs, fit the available lot space, and be in keeping with the style of the house.*

Materials Required: *A 1/4-in. scale ruler, design guides, floor plan of the existing house, larger sheet of tracing paper, larger sheet of squared drawing paper, pencils, eraser, colored pencil, drafting tape*

Note: Since the addition will be all new work, the plan will have to be drawn as for new construction. Many of the projects in Chapter 9, starting on Page 117, contain instructions to help you with this task.

MEASURING AND DRAWING THE EXTERIOR FOR AN ADDITION

It will be helpful to make drawings of the exterior that show how the new work will look. The information given in **Project 30**, "Drawing Elevations," will show you how to draw exterior (elevation) views of the home.

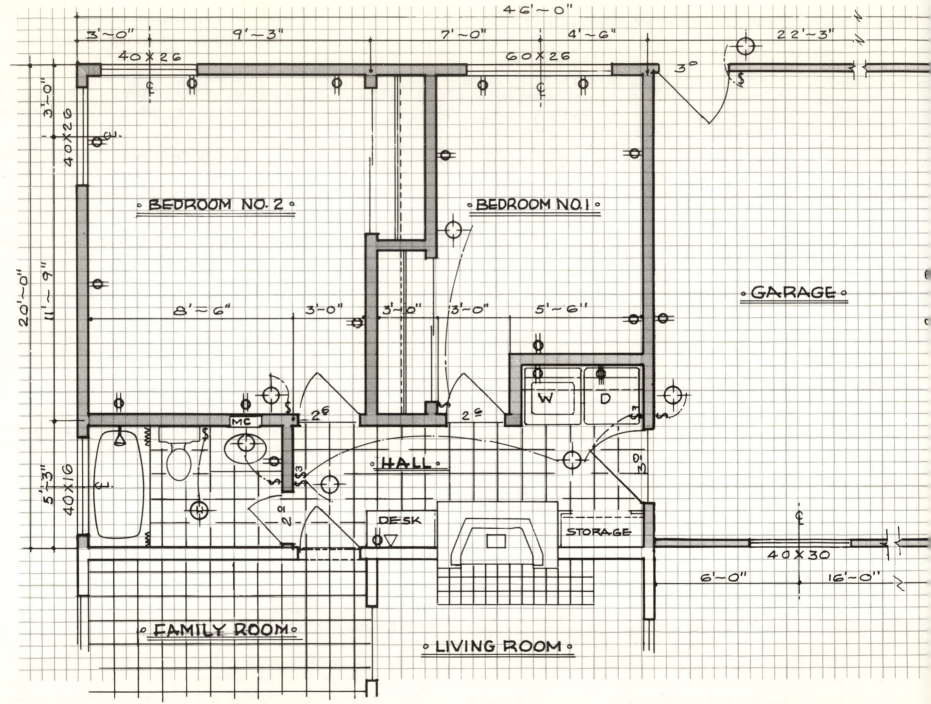

Figure 128. A plan for an addition to an existing house

150

PROJECT 28   Drawing The Exterior
Of The House

Objective: *To prepare drawings of the exterior of the existing house that will reveal the effect of the new addition on the overall appearance of the home.*

Materials Required: *A 1/4-in. scale ruler, the floor plan, sheet of squared drawing paper, tracing paper of equal size, pencil, eraser, drafting tape*

HOW TO MEASURE AND DRAW THE EXTERIOR:

1. Measure the house by following the instructions given in **Project 23**, "Drawing a Floor Plan of an Existing House," **Page 138**.

2. Add the new work when you have completed your elevation drawings of the existing house. To do this, cover the drawing with tracing paper and trace each side. These drawings will reveal to you the effect the new work will have on the appearance of the existing house.

3. Experiment with several different roof plans and exterior finish materials. See **Figs. 150-159**. Make as many drawings as necessary to achieve a pleasing effect.

4. Draw the new work accurately over your drawing of the existing house. The lines used to represent the existing house should be lighter than those representing the addition. See **Fig. 129**.

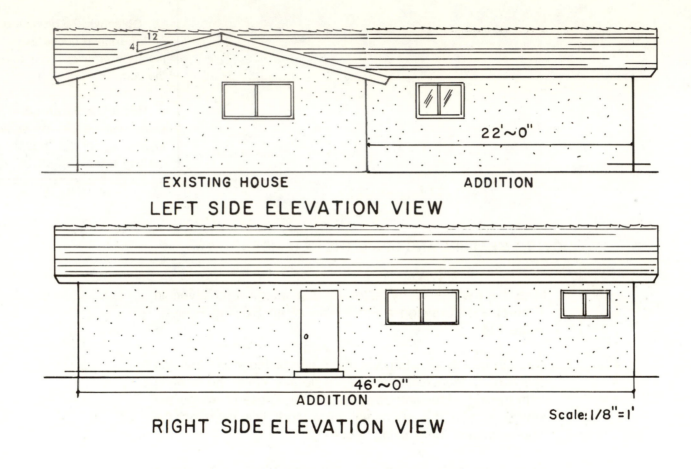

Figure 129.   Right and left side elevation views of an existing house showing a proposed addition.

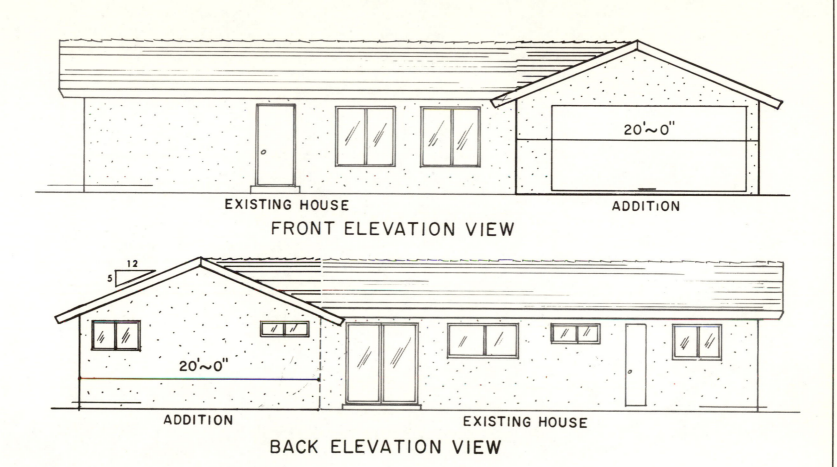

FRONT ELEVATION VIEW

BACK ELEVATION VIEW

Figure 129a.   Front and back elevation views of an existing house showing a proposed addition.

CHAPTER THIRTEEN

CONSTRUCTION TERMS, METHODS AND PROCEDURES

PROJECT 29   **Become Familiar With A Few Simple Construction Terms, Methods and Procedures**

UNDERSTANDING WOOD FRAMING CONSTRUCTION

It will help in planning a house if you study **Figs. 130-133**, to gain some understanding of the way homes are constructed. The numbers on the various parts of the structure are keyed to their definitions. The definitions are to be found on the following pages.

It is suggested that you look at some houses under construction while you are drawing plans. See if you can identify framing members by name. You may also pick up some interesting new ideas that could be incorporated in your plan.

CONSTRUCTION METHODS

Methods of construction vary widely. The method employed depends on the type of material used, such as wood frame or masonry (cement block or brick). The design of the building, the climate of the area, and the region of the country are all determining factors.

The information in this section is planned to give you an understanding of some of the more commonly used methods and terms of **wood frame construction**.

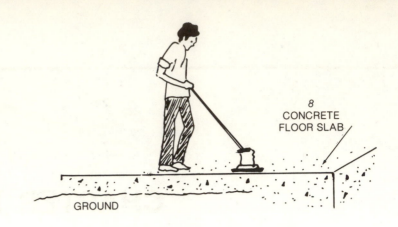

Figure 130.   Concrete floor slab.

Figure 131.   Floor-joist system.

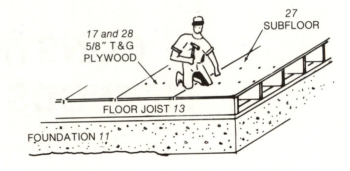

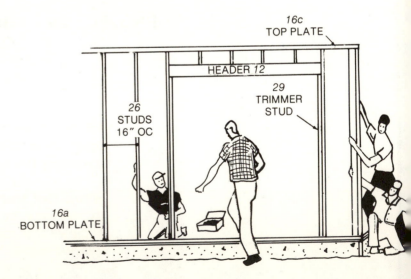

Figure 132.   Wood-frame construction.

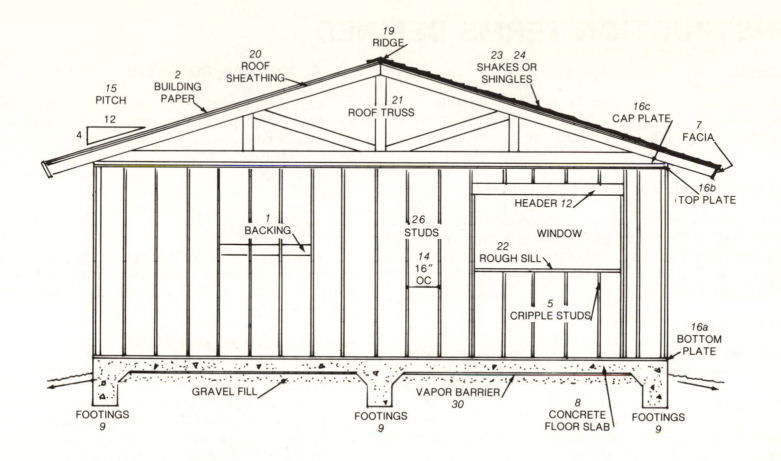

Figure 133.

NOTE: When roof trusses are used, the exterior walls upon which the trusses rest are called the bearing walls, (meaning the walls that carry the roof load).

When roof trusses are not used, it is common practice to use one or more of the interior partitions to help support the roof load and these walls are also called bearing walls.

CONSTRUCTION TERMS DEFINED

1. BACKING

Backing consists of 2- x 4-in. or 2- x 6-in. lumber nailed horizontally between studs to give solid support for anything that will be attached to finished walls, such as bathroom accessories, drapery rods, etc.

2. BUILDING PAPER, ASPHALT IMPREGNATED

This is a waterproof felt material, available in rolls of various widths and weights. Common applications are on roofs, under shingles or shakes, and as an underlayment for built-up roofs. It is also nailed onto the framework of the exterior walls of a wood frame house under stucco or siding.

3. BUILT-UP ROOF

This is a roof treatment that consists of multiple layers of asphalt-impregnated roofing felt, alternately mopped with heated, fluid tar.

4. CONCRETE

Concrete is a mixture of sand, gravel, and cement used for foundations, floors, patios, driveways, etc.

5. CRIPPLE STUD

This is a 2- x 4-in. framing member that has been cut off to fit below or above a framed opening in an exterior or interior wall.

6. EAVES

Eaves are the lower, horizontal portion of the roof that overhangs or projects beyond the exterior walls.

7. FACIA

This is a flat board, usually 2 x 6 in., 2 x 8 in., or 2 x 10 in., which is nailed onto the ends of the overhanging rafters. The facia is used for trim effect and can be an important element in the design.

8. FLOOR SLAB, CONCRETE

A slab of concrete creates a floor. This slab covers and becomes a part of the footings. As a general rule, a concrete floor slab is 4 in. thick and is poured over 4 in. of gravel, a vapor barrier, and steel mesh for reinforcing. When a floor slab is used, the ground must be graded to slope away from the house to drain water away from the foundation.

9. FOOTINGS

A footing is the concrete supporting base of the foundation wall. Footings are placed in undisturbed ground and extend to a depth below the frost line. Their purpose is to support the house and prevent settling.

10. FOUNDATION, BASEMENT

The basement foundation consists of reinforced walls, generally of concrete of sufficient thickness to resist the lateral forces of the earth. They are formed and poured in the excavated area. The wall thickness is determined by existing conditions. The footings are usually poured at the same time. A concrete floor is usually poured after the forms for the foundation walls have been removed.

11. FOUNDATION, CRAWL-SPACE

For a crawl-space foundation a wall is constructed on top of the footings in instances where a floor-joist system is to be used. It can be of concrete and poured at the same time as the footings, or of cement block or brick. The average foundation wall is installed so that there is 18 in. of crawl space between the bottom of the floor joist and the ground. With this system, pipes and heating and cooling ducts can be installed underneath the floor.

12. HEADER

A header is a beam placed above a framed opening for a window, door, closet, fireplace, etc. The header size is determined by the width of the opening and the weight that it will carry.

13. JOISTS

Joists are the beams used in a floor-joist system to support the floors.

14. ON CENTER

The words "on center," abbreviated **OC** when used in reference to 2- x 4-in. framing, mean that measurements are given from the center of one framing member to the center of the next. For example, studs are usually spaced at 16 in. **OC.**

15. PITCH

Pitch is the angle of incline of a roof. See **Fig. 141** on **Page 169**.

16. PLATES

There are three framing members described as plates:

(a) **Bottom plate**: The bottom horizontal member of a framed wall or partition (sometimes called a **sole plate**).

(b) **Top Plate:** The top horizontal member of a framed wall or partition.

(c) **Cap plate:** After the framed walls and partitions are in place, the cap plate is installed, It is nailed to the top plate in such a way as to tie all wall and partition framing together.

17. PLYWOOD

Plywood is a sheet of laminated wood, usually 4 ft. x 8 ft., but available in longer lengths. It is made of three or more layers of veneer (thin wood) laminated (glued) together. It is available in several thicknesses and in a tongue-and-groove pattern. It is used as sheathing on roofs and over floor joints as subflooring. It is also used in some instances on exterior walls as sheathing and for shear panels.

18. RAFTERS

When a roof is hand-framed (a truss is not used), a series of structural members, called rafters, are used to form the skeleton of the roof.

19. RIDGE

This is the horizontal line of the top edge of a roof where the two sloping sides meet.

20. ROOF SHEATHING

When plywood is nailed over roof framing, it is called roof sheathing. Roofing materials are applied over it.

21. ROOF TRUSS

Roof trusses are prefabricated roof framing. They can be fabricated for the individual house. They are made up and delivered to the job and hoisted into place on the roof. On the job carpenter work is minimized by this process and structurally accurate roof framing is achieved. The cost is usually about the same as for hand-framing.

22. ROUGH SILL

The horizontal framing member at the bottom of a window opening is the rough sill.

23. SHAKES

Shakes are similar to shingles, but are thicker and longer. They are usually of cedar or redwood and are rough in texture. They are available in medium and heavy weights and give a massive rustic look to a house.

24. SHINGLES

Shingles are uniformly shaped, individual pieces of roofing material that are nailed to the roof sheathing (either strips of wood called skip sheathing, or solid plywood) in overlapping rows. The term is used to cover a wide variety of types of roofing materials, such as wood, asphalt, slate, ceramic, asbestos, etc. Shingles of various types are also used as siding for special effects.

25. SIDING

Most materials, other than stucco or masonry, which are used to cover the outside walls of a wood framed house are called siding. Materials commonly used are various types of wood, manufactured in sheets measuring 4 ft. in width by 8, 9, or 12 ft. in length, or boards to be installed either horizontally, vertically, or diagonally. Aluminum or vinyl products and various types of shingles are also suitable siding materials.

26. STUDS

Studs in wood framing are usually 2 in. x 4 in. They are used to frame exterior walls and interior partitions. Studs are usually spaced at 16 in. **OC**, which means they are spaced 16 in. apart when measuring from the center of one stud to the center of the next. In some areas building codes approve 24 in. **OC** spacing in residential frame construction.

27. SUBFLOOR

This is a floor nailed on top of the floor joists to form a rigid base for finish flooring such as asphalt, vinyl tile, or carpet. **T & G** (tongue-and-groove) plywood is often used for this purpose.

28. TONGUE AND GROOVE

Tongue-and-groove is abbreviated **T&G**. Some plywood, planking, siding, and insulation boards are specially finished on the long side so that they will fit together. There is a tongue on one edge which fits into a corresponding groove on the adjoining sheet.

29. TRIMMER STUDS

Trimmer studs are the short 2- x 4-in. studs which support each end of a header.

30. VAPOR BARRIER

A vapor barrier is material used to prevent moisture penetration. Sheet plastic, such as polyurethane, is usually used when a vapor barrier is required beneath a concrete floor slab or outside of basement walls.

CHAPTER FOURTEEN

DRAWING PLANS FOR THE EXTERIOR OF A HOME

WHAT ARE ELEVATION DRAWINGS?

Elevations of a house are drawings that show the vertical details of the exterior. From them, one can learn what the proposed house would look like. A separate drawing is made for each side of the house.

The following information is conveyed by, or noted on, elevation drawings:

Roof: Shape, style, pitch, and roofing materials to be used.

Height: One story, two stories, split level, etc.

Windows and Doors: Appearance, style, placement, and height.

Wall Treatment: Stucco, siding, brick, cement block, or combined materials.

Trim: Placement, design, and materials to be used.

Floor System: Height of the finished floor from the ground line, dependent on the floor system used. See **Fig. 130**, **131**, and **133**.

Before starting to draw the elevation views of the home, you should have a mental picture of what the home should look like. The illustrations and front elevation views, **Figs. 150-159**, show many roof styles and exterior treatments. They may serve as a guide in deciding on the exterior treatment to be used.

HOW ARE ELEVATION VIEWS DRAWN?

In **Fig. 134**, each of the four sides of a house is shown pictorially. The **A**, **B**, **C**, and **D**, portions of the drawing are elevation views. The following instructions are given for drawing elevation views of a house with a simple gable roof design as shown in **Fig. 134**.

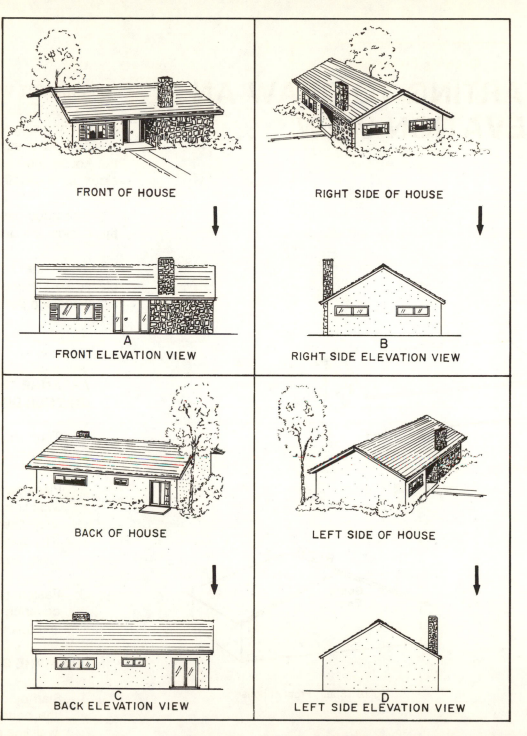

FRONT OF HOUSE

RIGHT SIDE OF HOUSE

A
FRONT ELEVATION VIEW

B
RIGHT SIDE ELEVATION VIEW

BACK OF HOUSE

LEFT SIDE OF HOUSE

C
BACK ELEVATION VIEW

D
LEFT SIDE ELEVATION VIEW

163

Figure 134.   The A, B, C, and D portions of the drawing are elevation views.

STARTING TO DRAW AN ELEVATION VIEW

EXPERIMENT WITH A GABLE ROOF DESIGN

When using a gable roof you have two choices: The roof can be constructed in such a way that the ridge is **parallel** with the front of the house; consequently the gables (peaked ends) are on the two sides, as shown in **Fig. 135**.

The ridge can also run from **front to back**, as in **Fig. 135a.** With this design, the gable ends face the front and back of the house.

When the house is rectangular in shape, trusses are usually placed so that they span the two narrow sides of the rectangle. This simple design permits the use of standardized prefabricated trusses.

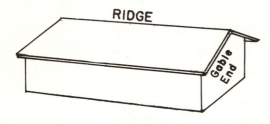

Figure 135.   Front of house.

ARRANGE THE FLOOR PLAN DRAWING ON YOUR DRAWING SURFACE:

1. Turn your floor-plan drawing so that one of the ends, where the gable end is to be, is facing you.

2. Place the drawing on your drawing surface so that the exterior wall line of the floor plan, which is facing you, is about half-way down on your drawing surface; then fasten it securely. The back half of the floor-plan drawing will probably hang over the back of your drawing surface. See **Fig. 136**.

3. Fasten tracing paper on the lower half of the board, just covering the floor-plan wall line. Follow the steps given on the following pages to draw the selected view of the house.

DRAW THE BOTTOM PLATE:

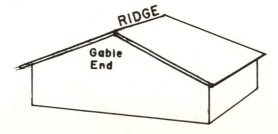

Figure 135a.   Front of house.

1. Start by drawing a light line on your tracing paper to represent the bottom of the wall (bottom plate) about 6 in. *below* the wall line on your floor plan. See **Fig. 137**.

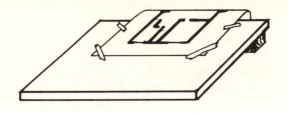

Figure 136.   Set up the drawing.

Step 1

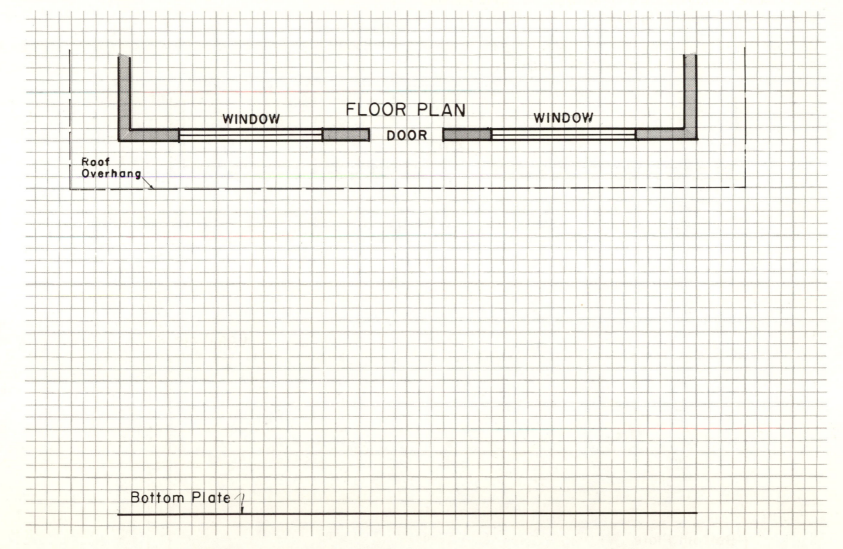

WINDOW   FLOOR PLAN   WINDOW

DOOR

Roof
Overhang

Bottom Plate

Figure 137.   Draw a line to represent the bottom of the bottom plate.

DRAW THE CAP PLATE:

1. Draw light projection (connecting) lines *down* from the outside corners of the floor plan allowing them to intersect with the bottom-plate line. See **Fig. 138**.

2. Measure *up* from the bottom plate line 8ft. - 1 1/2 in., in 1/4-in. scale, and draw a line to represent the top of the wall (cap plate) as shown in **Fig. 138**.

3. Go over the portion of the line that represents the outside corners of the wall with a heavier pressure on your lead.

Figure 138.
Measure the wall height and draw the top of the cap plate; then draw the corner lines.

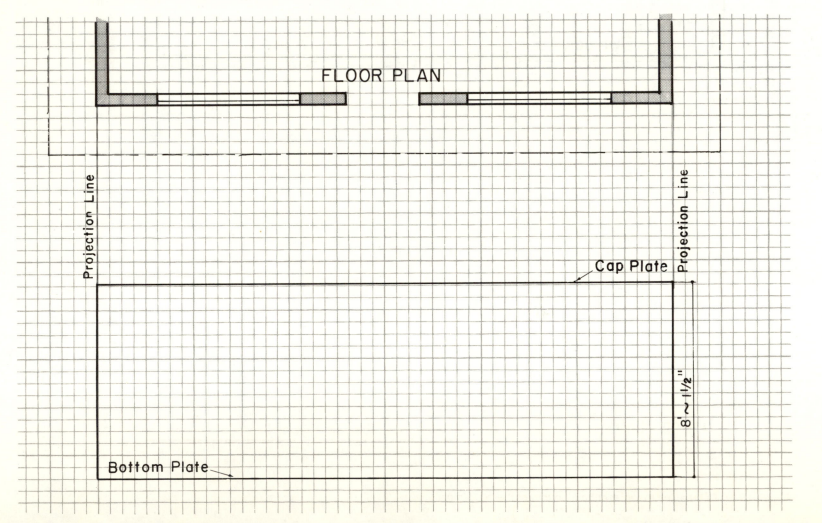

FLOOR PLAN

Projection Line

Projection Line

Cap Plate

8' ~ 11½"

Bottom Plate

Step 2

CHOOSE A FLOOR SYSTEM:

Concrete-Slab Floor System

1. If the house is to have a concrete-slab floor system, as shown in **Fig. 130**, measure *down* 8 in. (in 1/4-in. scale) from the bottom-plate line and make a mark.

2. Draw a line that indicates the ground (called ground line) as shown in **Fig. 139a**.

Floor-Joist System

1. If the house is to have a wood-frame floor-joist system, as shown in **Fig. 131**, measure *down* approximately 2 ft. - 3 in. from the bottom-plate line and make a mark.

2. Draw the ground line, as in **Fig. 139b**.

Step 3

Figure 139. Select the floor system to be used and draw the ground line.

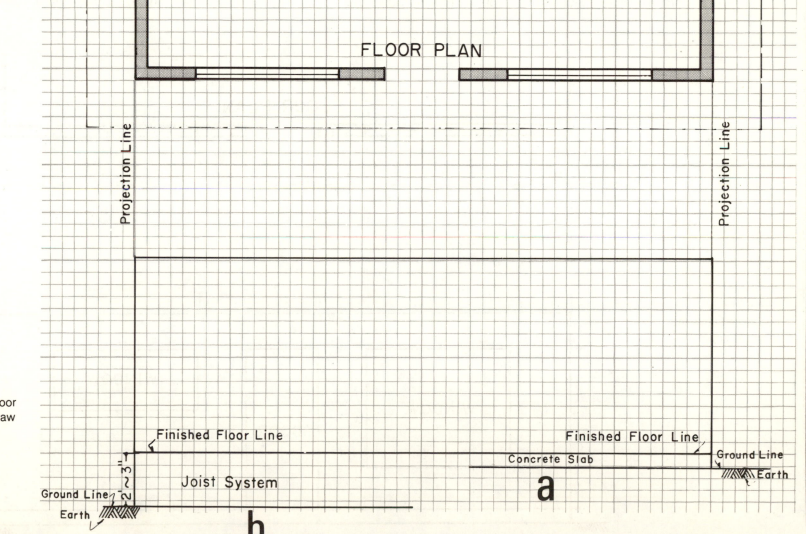

DRAW THE DOORS AND WINDOWS:

1. Measure *up* from the bottom-plate line 6 ft. - 8 in., in 1/4-in. scale, and draw a light *horizontal* line across the drawing to indicate the top of the doors and windows. See **Fig. 140**.

2. Extend light projection lines from the *outer* edge of each window and door on the floor plan through your elevation drawing, as shown in **Fig. 140**.

3. Check your floor plan for the height of each window. Measure *down*, from the line indicating the top of the window, the predetermined distance. Draw a line indicating the bottom of each window.

4. With a slightly heavier pressure on your pencil, draw *around* each window and door so that it is clearly distinguishable, as shown in **Fig. 140**.

5. Analyze the exterior appearance of the house. When drawing elevation views, it is often necessary to rearrange windows in order to improve the appearance. Be sure that changes are made so they do not spoil your interior room planning.

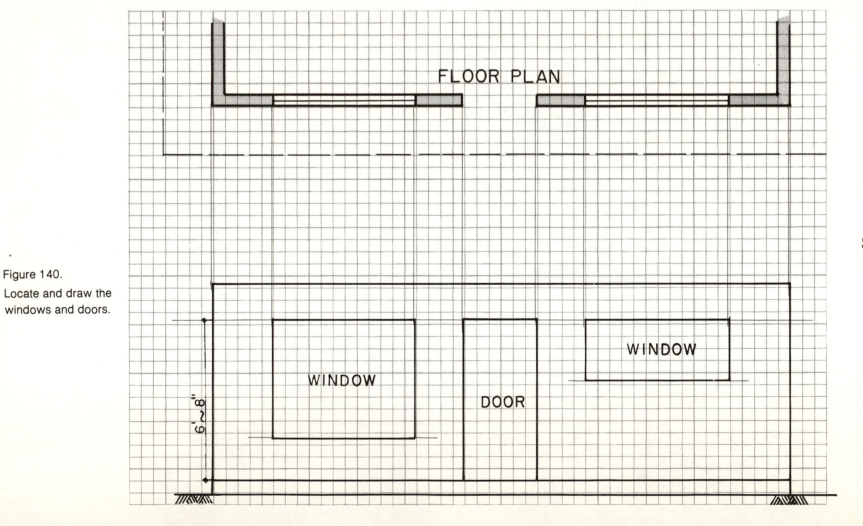

Figure 140.
Locate and draw the windows and doors.

Step 4

168

DESIGNING A GABLE ROOF

The appearance of a house is greatly affected by the kind, style, and slope of the roof. The roof design and materials you select should enhance the design of the home. However, weather conditions must also be taken into consideration. It is suggested that you observe the roofs on houses in your area. In most cases, they have been designed to withstand local weather conditions. If local weather conditions are extreme, research is needed to be sure the roof can withstand the maximum anticipated snow load.

ROOF PITCH

The word pitch means the angle of incline of a roof, or the slope. The degree of pitch is figured by increasing the angle of slope (or rise) 1 ft. for every 12 ft. of run. See **Fig. 141**.

NOTE: The pitch of a roof is expressed as: 1 in 12, 2 in 12, etc.

Figure 141.   How to figure the roof pitch.

NOTE: New materials and methods are continually increasing the flexibility of roof designing. It is best to check the manufacturers' specifications for the roofing material you plan to use before deciding on the exact slope of the roof.

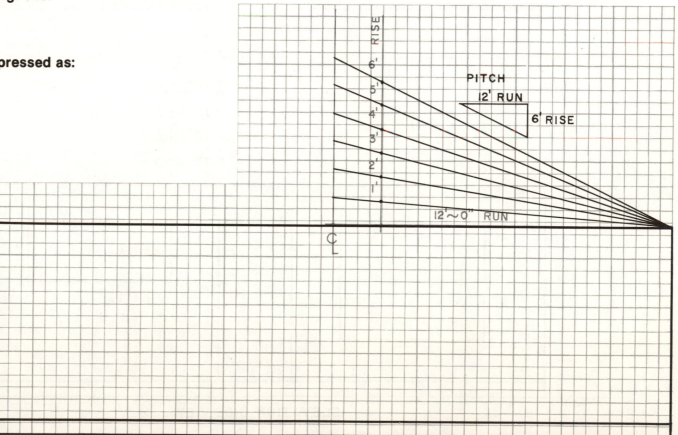

Step 5

MEASURING THE ROOF PITCH:

1. To construct a gable-roof design, begin by measuring *in* 12 ft. from one of the corner walls on your drawing, along the top of the cap plate and draw a light, *vertical* line, as shown in **Fig. 142.**

2. Measure *up* 1 ft. for each foot of rise, *dependent on the roof pitch selected*. Make a dot. See **Fig. 142.**

Figure 142.   Decide on and measure for the roof pitch.

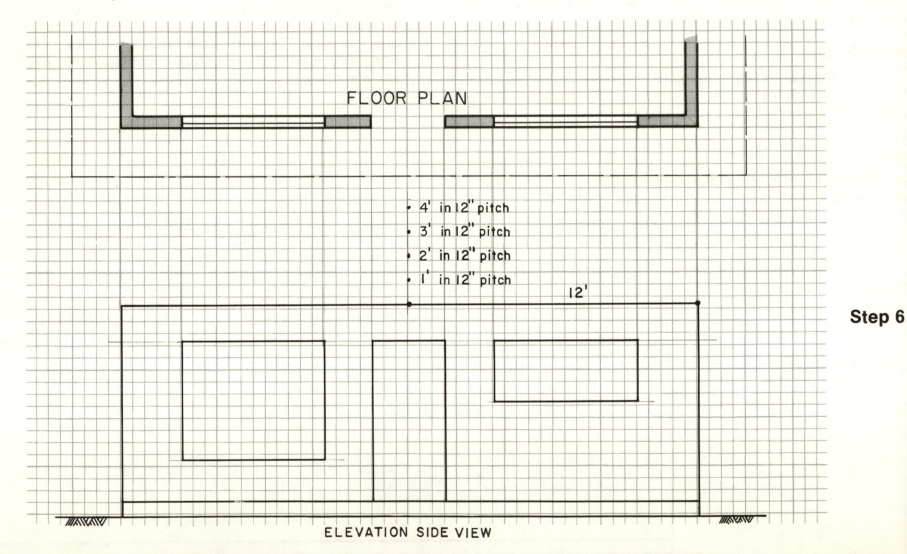

FLOOR PLAN

• 4' in 12" pitch
• 3' in 12" pitch
• 2' in 12" pitch
• 1' in 12" pitch

12'

ELEVATION SIDE VIEW

Step 6

DRAW THE ROOF ANGLE (PITCH):

1. Measure to locate the center of the wall.

2. Draw a light centerline *up* from the cap plate, as shown in **Fig. 143**.

3. Lay your triangle or straight edge on the drawing and connect the *top corner* of the wall with the dot on the 12 - ft. line.

4. If your building is to be wider than 24 ft., as shown in **Fig. 141** on **Page 169**, extend the line *at the same angle* to intersect with the centerline.

NOTE: In this example the 12 - ft. mark happens to be the center of the wall. This is not always the case.

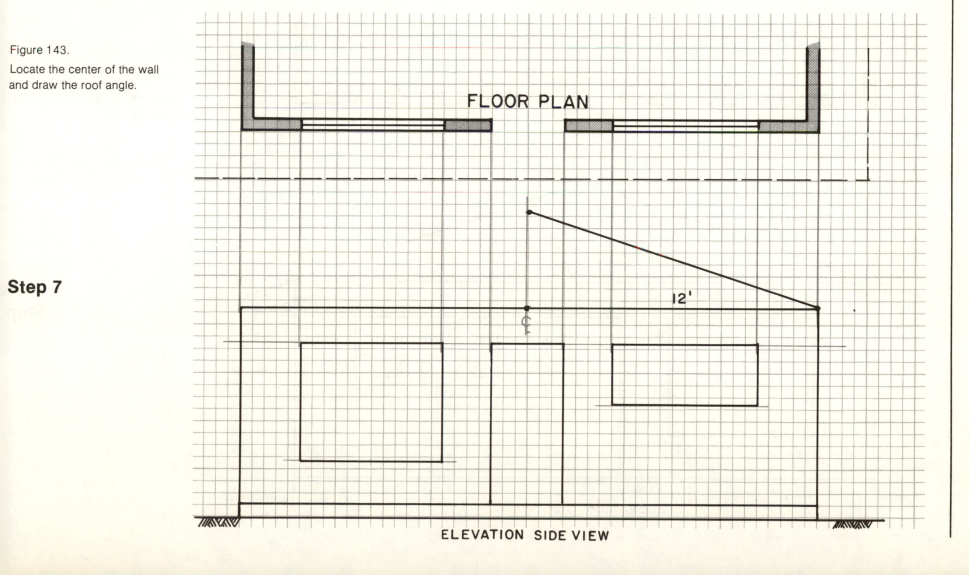

Figure 143.

Locate the center of the wall and draw the roof angle.

Step 7

FLOOR PLAN

12'

ELEVATION SIDE VIEW

171

COMPLETE THE GABLE END:

1. Draw a line from the top of the *opposite outside wall* to the established top of the gable, completing the gable end. **Fig. 133** on **Page 157**, shows the way a roof truss, or roof framing, rests on the top plates. Notice, on the same drawing, the way the eaves, or overhanging ends of trusses, appear on a drawing.

2. Roof framing usually projects beyond the walls of the structure, creating eaves. The amount of overhang varies, depending on the design and local weather conditions. Two feet of overhang is commonly used; however, more protection from sun and weather is obtained by using increased widths. Measure *out* from the wall corners, on both sides of the elevation, for the preferred amount of overhang and extend the lines of the roof, as shown in **Fig. 144**.

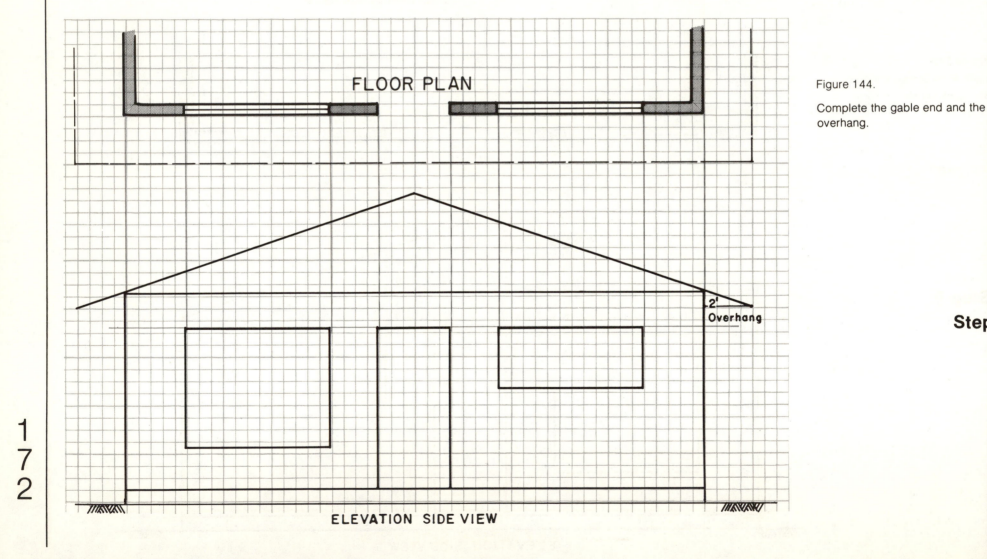

FLOOR PLAN

ELEVATION SIDE VIEW

2'
Overhang

Figure 144.

Complete the gable end and the overhang.

Step

172

DRAW FINISHING DETAILS:

1. Draw any details of trim, such as shutters, wood frames around windows, planter boxes, brick facing, etc.

2. If facia board is to be used for trim effect, draw it as shown in **Fig. 145**. Facia boards are usually 1 or 2 in. thick by 6, 8, or 10 in. wide, depending on the desired appearance. They are often of redwood.

3. Draw designations to indicate the material to be used for the exterior finish, such as stucco, wood siding, brick, etc. Refer to the symbol chart for exterior finishing materials, **Fig. 146**.

Figure 145.
Draw the finishing details.

Step 9

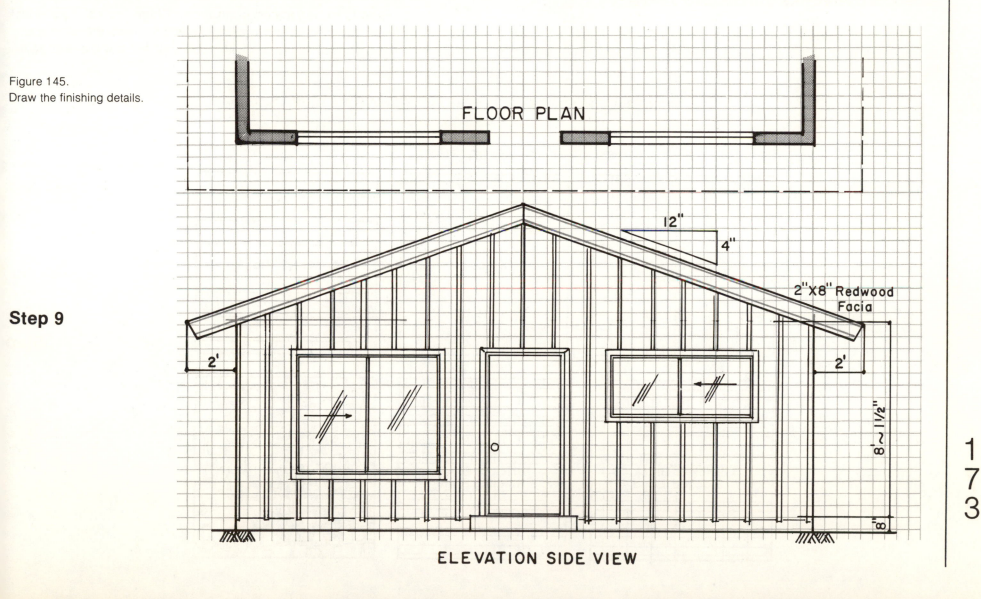

FLOOR PLAN

12"

4"

2"X8" Redwood Facia

2'

2'

8'~11/2"

8"

ELEVATION SIDE VIEW

SELECTING ROOFING MATERIALS

The roofing materials used most frequently are listed below.

Built-up roof is a roof treatment that consists of multiple layers of asphalt impregnated roofing felt, alternately mopped with heated tar. Sometimes crushed rock is applied over the final coat.

The term **shingles** is used to cover a wide variety of types of roofing materials, such as wood, asphalt, slate, ceramic, asbestos, etc.

New materials and methods are continually increasing the flexibility of roof designing. It is best to check the manufacturer's specifications for the roofing material you plan to use before deciding on the exact slope of the roof.

If the home is to be located in an area of high fire risk, consider flammability of materials when making selections and the increased insurance rates applied to homes with roofs that are not fire-retardant.

POSSIBLE CHOICES FOR EXTERIOR FINISHING MATERIALS:

Figure 146.   Symbols to represent exterior wall-finishing materials.

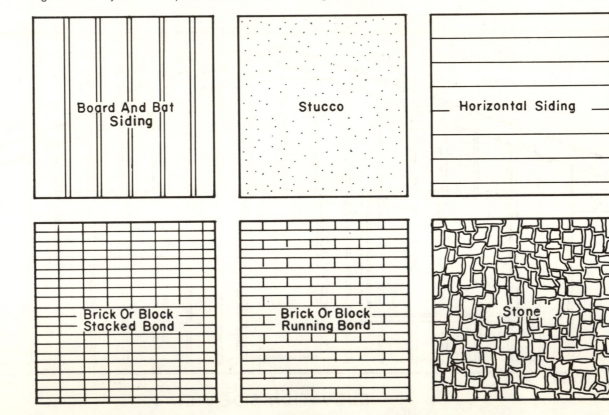

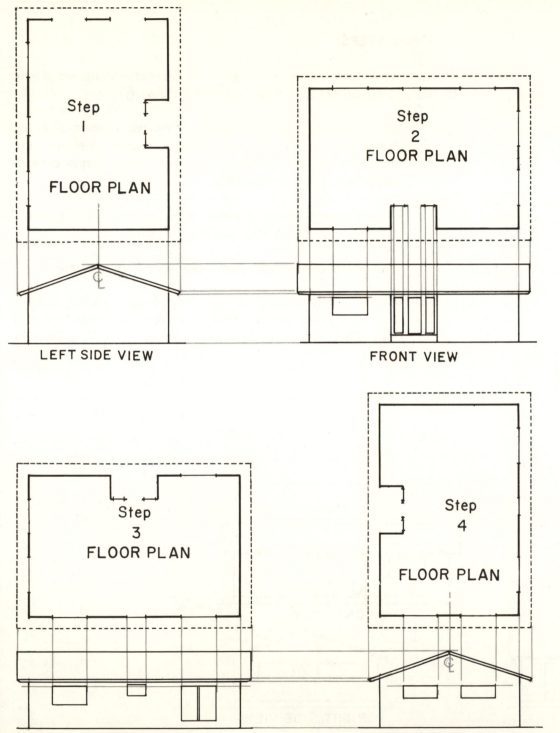

Step 1
FLOOR PLAN

LEFT SIDE VIEW

Step 2
FLOOR PLAN

FRONT VIEW

Step 3
FLOOR PLAN

BACK VIEW

Step 4
FLOOR PLAN

RIGHT SIDE VIEW

PROJECT 31   Constructing Elevation Views For Each Side Of The House

Objective: *To draw elevation views of the house that match the first drawing and show the details of the other views.*

Materials Required: *A 1/4-in. scale ruler, your floor plan and front elevation view, larger sheet of squared drawing paper, tracing paper of equal size, pencil, eraser, drafting tape*

Figure 147.

DRAWING VIEWS OF ALL FOUR SIDES:

1. Place the floor plan on your working surface, as in **Fig. 136**, with the side to be drawn facing you.

2. Draw the elevation view, using the vertical measurements already established on your first elevation view. See **Steps 1** and **2** in **Fig. 147**.)

3. Continue to turn the floor plan around and draw an elevation view for the other two sides of the house as in **Steps 3** and **4** in **Fig. 147**.

NOTE: When drawing a simple gable roof design, the highest point of the gable, as established in your first drawing, will be the height of the ridge in all views.

175

FINAL STEPS:

When all four views have been drawn individually on tracing paper, you will be ready to make a finished drawing.

1. With scissors, trim the surplus tracing paper, then align and fasten the four elevation views to your working surface in a neat arrangement that will fit on your large sheet of drawing paper, as shown in **Fig. 148.**

2. Place the large sheet of paper over the elevation views and fasten it securely to your working surface.

3. Trace each view sharply and neatly and draw in all the details.

4. Write in any necessary notations and dimensions. By studying the illustrations and accompanying elevation drawings, **Fig. 150-159**, you can see how this is done.

Figure 148.   Arrangement of elevation views.

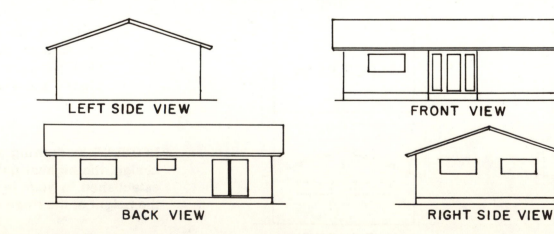

LEFT SIDE VIEW   FRONT VIEW

BACK VIEW   RIGHT SIDE VIEW

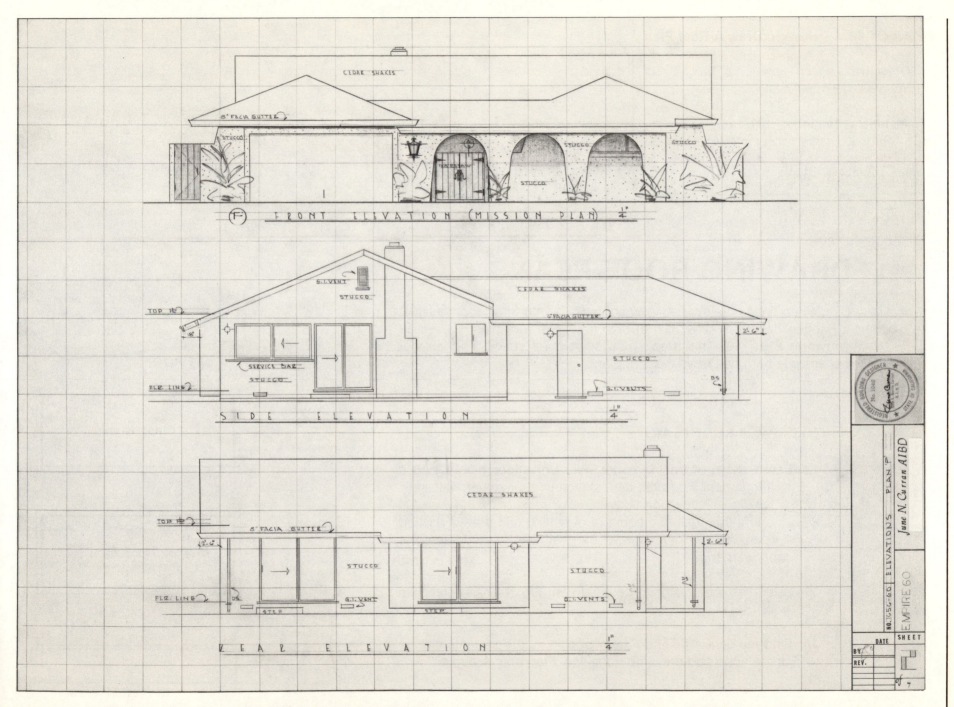

Fig. 148a.   Example drawing of completed elevation views.

Objective: *To learn how to construct a roof plan for the chosen roof design.*

Materials Required: *A 1/4-in. scale ruler, your floor plan, larger sheet of tracing paper, pencil, eraser, drafting tape. For a hip roof: a 45° triangle; see Fig. 8, Item G*

DRAWING ROOF PLANS

When drawing elevation views of houses with other roof designs, it is often helpful to draw a roof plan first. The roof plan is used as shown in **Fig. 149**. This drawing is for your reference, and will not necessarily be a part of your set of plans.

TO DRAW A ROOF PLAN:

1. Lay a sheet of tracing paper over your floor plan. Using a soft lead pencil or a felt pen, sketch in the exterior wall lines.

2. Measure the desired amount of overhang and draw a dashed line around the perimeter of the wall lines to represent the roof overhang.

3. Select the roof design to be used from **Fig. 149** and complete your roof plan as shown.

4. Find the center point on the roof plan that represents the top of the ridge and draw the ridge line. *Flat roofs excepted*.

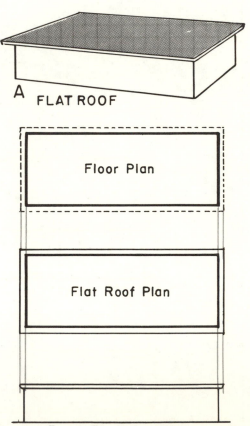

A FLAT ROOF

Floor Plan

Flat Roof Plan

Front Elevation View

Figure 149.   Drawings of other roof designs.

DRAWING ELEVATION VIEWS FROM ROOF PLANS:

Figure 149, Designs **A**, **B**, **C**, and **D**, shows the procedure to follow when constructing elevation views from roof plans.

1. Referring to the roof design for which you have drawn a roof plan, **Fig. 149**, draw extension lines *down* from each corner of the wall lines. Then complete the elevation view.

2. Proceed to draw an elevation view of each side of the house as shown in **Steps 1-9**, **Pages 165-173**.

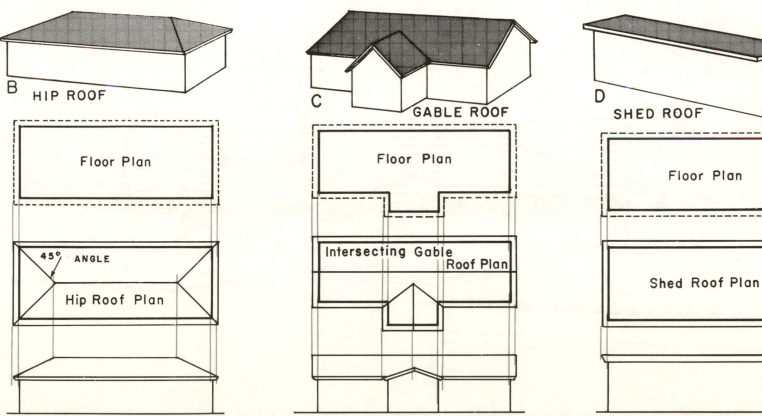

B HIP ROOF

Floor Plan

45° ANGLE

Hip Roof Plan

Front Elevation View

C GABLE ROOF

Floor Plan

Intersecting Gable
            Roof Plan

Front Elevation View

D SHED ROOF

Floor Plan

Shed Roof Plan

Front Elevation View

180

Figure 150.   The roof over the main part of the house in this drawing is a gable design. The intersecting roof on the wings is called a hip.

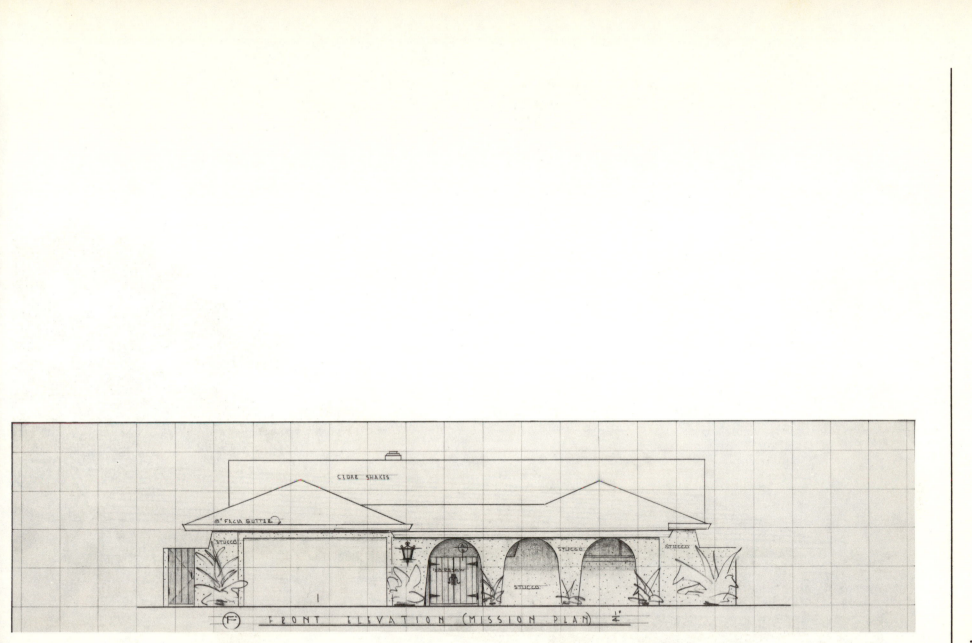

Figure 151.   Front elevation view of Fig. 150.

182

Figure 152.   The roof design on this house is a simple gable.

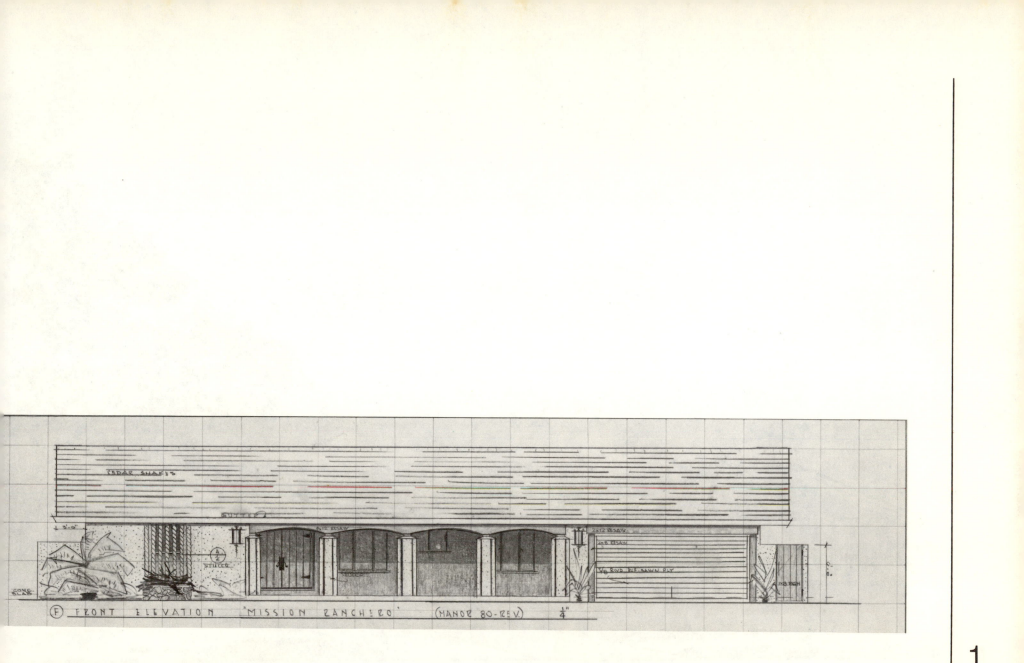

Figure 153.   Front elevation view of Fig. 152.

Figure 154.   This is a gable roof design with an intersecting gable on the wing.

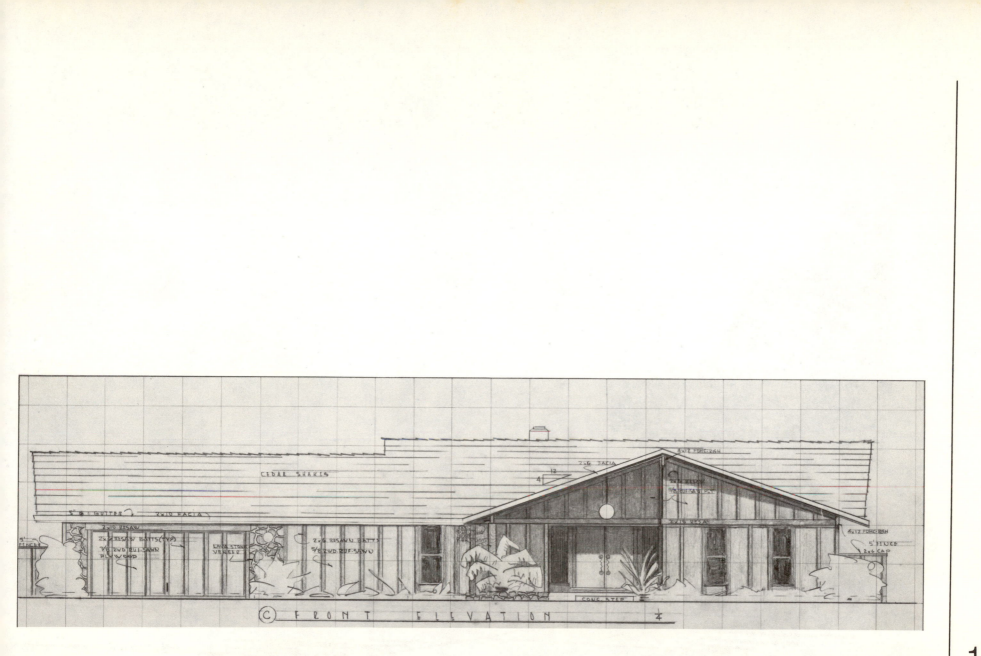

Figure 155.   Front elevation view of Figure 154.

186

Figure 156.   A gable roof design with two intersecting gables.

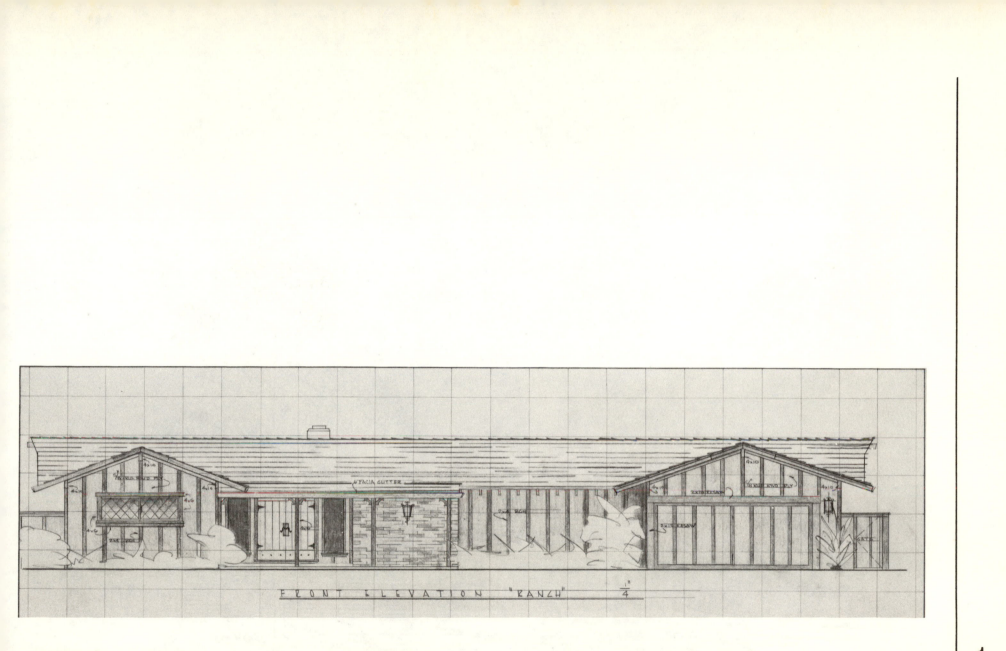

Figure 157. Front elevation view of Fig. 156.

Figure 158.   A gable roof design on the main part of the house with two intersecting hip roof designs on the two wings.

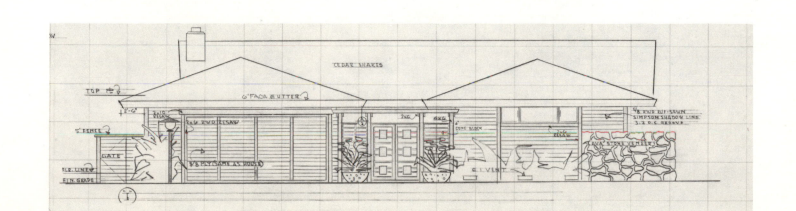

Figure 159.   Front elevation view of Fig. 158.

CHAPTER FIFTEEN

HOW TO OBTAIN A SET OF PRINTS

PROJECT 35   **Making Copies Of Your Drawings**

WHAT IS AN ORIGINAL?

Everything you draw when drawing plans for a home, whether it is a sketch or a carefully detailed and scaled drawing, is considered to be an *original*.

I have suggested throughout this book that you make your original drawings only on translucent paper. There are two reasons for this. First, it is frequently necessary to trace drawings. Translucent paper makes this task much easier. Second, good inexpensive copies are obtained from drawings made on translucent paper.

House plan drawings must be reviewed by the government agencies issuing building permits, the lending institutions making loans on property, individuals involved with constructing the house, and those who will figure the required building materials. Obviously, fragile original drawings cannot withstand handling. So much time and thought go into original drawings that one cannot risk having them lost or defaced. Being handed an original drawing would also make a very poor impression on an individual in the building industry.

WHERE TO OBTAIN PRINTS

Almost all cities and even most small towns have a printer who is equipped to copy your original drawings for a surprisingly low price. Look in the yellow pages of your telephone directory under "Blue Printers."

WHAT ARE BLUEPRINTS?

For many years the most commonly used method of making prints of house plans was blueprinting. This is a process in which the original drawing is fed into a machine along with a piece of sensitized blueprint paper. After exposure to a light source, the print goes through a wet process. The resulting copy is exactly like the original drawing except that it is, as its name implies, blue in color. The lines from your original drawing appear on the blueprint as white. It is in effect a blue negative print. This type of print is very durable. It can withstand weather and rough handling on the job.

WHAT ARE WHITEPRINTS?

Another method of making a print from an original is called whiteprinting or diazo. By this process an exact copy is made from an original. A whiteprinter is a small, uncomplicated machine. The type of translucent paper used in this system is similar to that used in blueprinting. The original, along with a piece of sensitized paper, is fed into the machine and exposed to light. The print is then passed through a chamber and the image is developed by ammonia vapor. The resulting print is white. The linework on the original appears as blue on the print. The print is a positive copy of the original. This method is fast and inexpensive. You can make notations and changes on a whiteprint copy, as pencil marks show up clearly. However, the blue lines will in time fade when the print is exposed to weather.

Although white paper with blue lines is most commonly used for house plans, a variety of paper and image colors are sensitized for use in whiteprinters.

NONREPRODUCIBLE BLUES

Certain shades of blue *do not* reproduce by either the blueprinting or whiteprinting method of reproduction. The lines on the squared translucent drawing paper have been printed with one of these nonreproducible blues. Consequently, when prints are made from drawings on this type of paper, the blue lines do not appear on the print. Squares have been printed on drawing paper for convenience in preparing plans only.

Most stationery and drafting supply stores carry a special blue pencil called a *nonrepro pencil*. This pencil is handy for marking notations and calculations on the drawing that are not to appear on the print.

LINEWORK AND REPRODUCTION QUALITY

The appearance and legibility of a print will depend to a certain extent upon the quality of linework on the original drawing. It is suggested that you make a letter-sized sample on squared drawing paper of different line weights drawn in the grades of lead you have been using on your plans. It will cost only a few cents to have a print made of this sample. From this you can tell how your work will show up in a print.

HOW SHADED LINES REPRODUCE

The ordinary blue colored pencil, recommended for shading lines which indicate wood frame walls, *will* show up in a print. Include on your sample some shading done with whatever colored pencils you have available; select the best one, as revealed by the print, for all your shading work.

ABBREVIATIONS

A

Access Door	AD
Access Panel	AP
Acoustic	ACST
Acoustical Plaster	ACST PLAS
Acoustical Tile	AT
Addition	ADD.
Air Conditioning	AIR COND
Area	A
Asbestos	ASB
Asphalt	ASPH
Asphalt Tile	AT
At	@
Automatic	AUTO
Avenue	AVE

B

Bathroom	B
Bath Tub	BT
Beam	BM
Bearing	BRG
Bedroom	BR
Blocking	BLKG
Blueprint	BP
Boundary	BDY
Brick	BRK
British Thermal Units	BTU
Broom Closet	BC
Building	BLDG
Building line	BL
Base Cabinet	B CAB
Built-in	BLT-IN
Burglar Alarm	BA
Button	BUT.
Buzzer	BUZ
By (as 6' X 8')	X

C

Cabinet	CAB.
Ceiling	CLG
Cement	CEM
Cement Floor	CEM FL
Center	CTR
Centerline	CL
Center to Center	C to C
Centers On	OC
Cesspool	CP
Circuit Breaker	CIR BKR
Cleanout	CO
Clock Outlet	C
Closet	C or CL or CLO
Clothes Pole	CP
Coat Closet	CC
Cold Water	CW
Concrete	CONC
Concrete Block	CONC B
Concrete Floor	CONC FL
Construction	CONST
Contractor	CONTR
Counter	CTR
Cubic Foot	CU FT
Curtain Rod	C R

D

Dimension	dim or DIM
Dining Room	D R
Dish Washer	DW
Door	DR
Double Glass	DG
Double Hung Window	DHW
Downspout	DS
Drain	D or DR
Drawing	DWG
Dryer	D

E

East	E
Electric	elec or ELEC
Electrical Panel	EP
Entrance	ENT
Emergency	EMER
Elevation	EL
Equipment	EQUIP.
Excavate	EXC
Exhaust	EXH
Existing	EXIST.
Exterior	EXT

F

Feet	(') FT
Figure	FIG.
Firebrick	FBRK
Fireproof	FPRF
Fire Place	FP
Fire Extinguisher	F EXT
Fixture	FIX.
Flashing	FL
Floor	FL
Floor Drain	FD
Flooring	FLG
Fluorescent	FLUOR
Foot	(') FT
Footing	FTG
Foundation	FDN
Frame	FR
Framing	Frm
Front	FR
Furnish	FURN

G

Garage	GAR
Garbage Disposal	G/D
Gas	G
Glass	GL
Gypsum	GYP

H

Hall	H
Hardware	HDW
Heater	HTR
Heater, water	wh
Height	HGT H or HT
Horizontal	HOR
Hose Bib	HB
Hot Water	HW
House	HSE

I

Inch	(") IN.
Include	INCL
Information	INFO
Insulate	INS
Intercommunication	INTERCOM
Interior	INT

K

Keyed Alike	KA
Kitchen	K

L

Laundry	LAU
Laundry Trays	LT
Length Over-all	LOA
Light	LT
Linen Closet	L CL
Linoleum	Lino
Linoleum Floor	LF
Living Room	LR
Louver	LV

M

Manufacture	MFR
Manufactured	MFD
Manufacturer	MFR
Material	MATL
Medicine Cabinet	MC
Medium	MED
Miscellaneous	MISC

N

North	N
Number	NO.

O

On Center	OC
Outlet	OUT
Over-all	OA
Overhead	OVHD

P

Painted	PTD
Panel	PNL
Pantry	PAN.
Partition	PTN
Plate	PL
Plate Glass	PL GL
Plumbing	PLMB
Porch	P
Prefabricated	PREFAB
Property	Prop
Proposed	PROP
Pull Chain	P or PC
Push Button	PB

R

Radiator	RAD
Radio	R
Range	R
Refrigerator	REF
Register	REG
Remove	REM
Repair	REP
Revision	REV
Roof	RF
Roofing	Rfg. or RFG
Room	RM or R
Rough	RGH
Round	RD

S

Safety	SAF
Scale	SC
Schedule	SCH
Section	SECT
Self-closing	SC
Service	SERV
Sewer	SEW.
Sewer, clay tile	S-CT
Sheathing	SHTHG
Sheet	SH
Shelves (as 2 shelves)	2 SH
Shower	SH
Shut Off Valve	SOV
Siding	Sdg or SDG
Sink	SK or S
Sketch	SK
South	S
Speaker	SPKR
Specifications	SPEC
Sprinkler	SPR
Square	SQ
Square Foot	sq ft' or ☐
Stained	stnd or STN
Stairs	ST
Standard	std or Std or STD
Storage	STG
Storage Closet	ST CL
Street	ST
Structural	STR
Switch	SW
Symbol	SYM

T

Telephone	TEL
Television	TV
Terra Cotta	TC
Terrazzo	TER
That is	ie or IE
Thermostat	THERMO
Toilet	T
Tongue And Groove	T&G
Typical	TYP

U

Unit Heater . . . . UH
Up . . . . U
Utility Room. . . . . UR

V

Vacuum. . . . . VAC
Vacuum Cleaning Line V
Valve. V
Vapor Proof. . . . . VAP. PRF
Vent. V
Vent Duct. . . . . VD
Vent Pipe . . . . VP
Vent Stack . . . . VS
Ventilate. . . . . VENT.
Vertical . . . . VERT

W

Wall Cabinet . . . . W CAB
Washing Machine. W
Watercloset . . . . WC
Water Heater . . . . wh
Water Line. . . . . WL
Weather Stripping . . . . WS
Weatherproof . . . . WP
West. . . . . W
Width . . . . W
Window. . . . . WDW
With. . . . . W/
Without . . . . W/O
Wood. . . . . WD
Wrought Iron . . . . WI

Y

Yard . . . . YD

197

OTHER USEFUL BOOKS

PLANNING, DESIGN, AND DRAFTING FOR HOMES

PROFILE YOUR LIFESTYLE
Questions To Ask Yourself Before Building, Buying Or Remodeling A Home
Curran, June
Brooks Publishing Company
930 Truxtun Avenue
Bakersfield, California 93301

ARCHITECTURAL DRAWING AND PLANNING
Goodban And Hayslett
McGraw-Hill Book Company
1221 Avenue of the Americas
New York, New York 10020

ARCHITECTURAL GRAPHICS
Ching, Frank
Van Nostrand Reinhold Company
New York

ARCHITECTURAL WORKING DRAWINGS
A Professional Technique
Thomas, Marvin L.
McGraw-Hill Book Company
New York, New York 10020

RESIDENTIAL DESIGNS
How To Get The Most For Your Housing Dollar
Link, David E.
Cahners Books
Division of Cahners Publishing Company, Inc.
89 Franklin Street, Boston, Massachusetts 02110

THINKING SOLAR AND ENERGY CONSERVATION

DESIGN FOR A LIMITED PLANET
Living With Natural Energy
Skurka And Naar
Ballantine Books
New York, New York

HOME ENERGY HOW-TO
Upgrade Your Home Insulation - Save On Your Present Heating And Cooling Systems - Produce Your Own Home Energy From Sun, Wind, Wood, Water, Biofuels
Hand, A.J.
Popular Science
Harper and Row
New York, New York

SOLAR DWELLING DESIGN CONCEPTS
The AIA Research Corporation
For sale by the Superintendent of Documents, U.S. Government Printing Office, Washington, D.C. 20402   Stock Number Is 023-000-00334-1

YOUR ENGINEERED HOUSE
Roberts, Rex
M. Evans and Company, Inc.
New York, New York 10017

HEATING

COMFORT HEATING
Langley, Billy C.
Reston Publishing Company, Inc.
(A Prentice-Hall Company)
Reston, Virginia 22090

GETTING THE MOST FOR YOUR HOUSING DOLLAR

BUILDING OR BUYING THE HIGH-QUALITY HOUSE AT LOWEST COST
A Practical Guide For A Family Making Its Largest Single Investment
Watkins, A.M.
Dolphin Books
Doubleday & Company, Inc.
Garden City, New York

HOME BUYER'S GUIDE
(Barnes and Noble Everyday Handbooks - No. 213)
Wren, Jack
Barnes & Noble, Inc.
New York, New York

LAWYERS TITLE HOME BUYING GUIDE
Laas, William M.
Popular Library
New York, New York

THE HOME OWNER'S SURVIVAL KIT
How To Beat The High Cost Of Owning And Operating Your Home
Watkins, A.M.
Hawthorne Books, Inc.
New York, New York

BUILDING AND CONSTRUCTION TERMS DEFINED

DICTIONARY OF ARCHITECTURE AND CONSTRUCTION
1775 Illustrations
Harris, Cyril M.
McGraw-Hill Book Company
1221 Avenue of the Americas
New York, New York 10020

ILLUSTRATED ENCYCLOPEDIC DICTIONARY OF BUILDING
AND CONSTRUCTION TERMS
Brooks, Hugh
Prentice-Hall, Inc.
Englewood Cliffs, New Jersey

HOME BUILDING

HOUSES

The Illustrated Guide To Construction, Design And Systems
Harrison, Henry S.
National Institute of Real Estate Brokers
of the National Association of Realtors
Chicago, Illinois

HOW TO BUILD YOUR OWN HOME
Building, Buying, And Accessories
Reschke, Robert C.
Structures Publishing Company 1976
Farmington, Michigan

HOW TO PLAN, BUY OR BUILD YOUR LEISURE HOME
Wicks, Harry
Reston Publishing Company, Inc.
(A Prentice-Hall Company)
Reston, Virginia 22090

WOOD-FRAME HOUSE CONSTRUCTION
Anderson, L.O.
Craftsman Book Company Of America
124 South La Brea, Los Angeles, California 90036

OBTAINING CONSTRUCTION FUNDS

CONSTRUCTION FUNDING
Where The Money Comes From
Halperin, Don A.
A Wiley-Interscience Publication
John Wiley & Sons
New York, New York

REMODELING AND RESTORATION

HOW TO REMODEL AND ENLARGE YOUR HOME
Daniels, M.E.
Bobbs-Merrill
Indianapolis, New York

REMODELING OLD HOUSES
Without Destroying Their Character
Stephen, George
Alfred A. Knopf, Inc.
New York, New York

THE COMPLETE BOOK OF HOME REMODELING
Scharff, Robert
McGraw-Hill Book Company
1221 Avenue of the Americas
New York, New York 10020

LANDSCAPING

LANDSCAPE DESIGN, Homeowner's Guide to
Michel, Timothy M.
The Countryman Press
Taftsville, Vermont

PRACTICAL GUIDE TO HOME LANDSCAPING
Readers Digest Association, Inc.
Pleasantville, New York 10570

GLOSSARY

For framing and other construction terms, see the illustrated glossary in Chapter 13.

ATRIUM
An inner court with an open space in the roof.

ATTIC
The space between the ceiling and the roof rafters.

BASEBOARD
A trim board applied after the finish floor has been installed to cover the joint where the floor and wall meet.

BEAM CEILING
A ceiling in which the beams are exposed. Sometimes called an exposed beam ceiling.

BEARING WALLS
Walls structurally capable of supporting the roof load.

BIFOLD DOORS
A door made up of pairs of narrow panels, hinged together.

BLUEPRINTS
A print made from an original translucent drawing.

BOARD AND BAT SIDING
A type of wall finishing for wood-frame houses. Boards or sheets of plywood are applied vertically. The joints are covered with narrow strips of wood called bats. They are usually spaced 16 in. or 24 in. on center.

BUILDING LINES
Dashed lines drawn on a plot plan of a lot to define the area within which a house or garage may be built; also referred to as setbacks.

BUILT-UP ROOF
A roof treated with layers of felt and asphalt, sometimes called a tar and felt roof.

CARPORT
A shelter for a car composed of a roof supported by corner posts. Some carports have storage walls in the end or along one side.

CASING
The visible trim or molding around a door or window.

CL (CENTER LINE)
A line that marks the center of any given space.

CLEANOUT HOLES
In a masonry fireplace, an opening in the bottom course, or in the floor of the firebox, for removal of ashes.

CRAWL SPACE
The space below the floor of a house usually enclosed by the foundation wall.

CROSS-SECTION PAPER
Drafting paper on which squares have been printed to indicate scale.

DIAZO PRINTING MACHINE
A machine used to make prints from drawings originally drawn on translucent paper such as vellum.

DIMENSION LINE
A line drawn for the purpose of indicating the distance between two points.

DIMENSIONING SYSTEM
A method of showing actual measurements on a drawing.

DIMENSIONS
Figures which indicate actual sizes on scale drawings.

DUCTS
Round, square, or oval shaped tubes used to conduct cooled or heated air to outlets in individual rooms; usually made of non-combustible material such as sheet metal.

EAVE
The lower edge of that portion of the roof which overhangs or projects beyond the exterior wall.

ELEVATIONS
Views of the exterior sides of a house or other structure.

EXTENSION LINE
Lines which extend from the exterior corners of a building to show the beginning and ending of a dimension line.

FACADE

The frontal treatment of a building.

FACE BRICK

Brick used to face a wall for decorative purposes.

FIREBOX

The portion of a fireplace that contains the fire. In masonry fireplaces it is lined with brick that has been hardened and made heat-resistant; called fire brick.

GLASS, INSULATING

Two pieces of glass spaced apart, about 1/4 in., and sealed to form a single unit with an air space between. This process is also called double glazing.

GLASS, LAMINATED OR SHATTER RESISTANT

A layer of clear plastic is fused between two sheets of glass to prevent shattering.

GLASS, OBSCURE

An opaque, decorative glass usually used in bathroom windows for privacy.

GLASS, PATTERN

A variety of designs and colors are used to make glass decorative, create privacy, or diffuse light.

GLASS, PLATE

Polished glass that is without the waves characteristic of sheet glass, varies in thickness from 1/8 to 1-1/4 in. thick.

GLASS, SAFETY

Laminated, tempered, and wire glass are all preferred for safety characteristics.

GLASS, SHEET

Sheet glass has a characteristic waviness. It comes in single strength (3/32-in. thick), double strength (1/8-in. thick), and heavy (3/16-in., 7/32-in., and 1/4-in.).

GLASS, TEMPERED

Glass which has been heat strengthened.

GRAPH PAPER

Drafting paper marked off in squares for use in scale drawing.

GUTTERS AND DOWN-SPOUTS

Troughs and pipes that carry rain water away from the house.

HEARTH

The noncombustible floor and area in front of a fireplace.

HEAT LOSS (OR GAIN) CALCULATIONS

Calculations made to determine the amount of heat transmission through exterior walls, windows, roof, or floors.

HOSE BIB

A water faucet, located on the outside of the house, with a fitting to which a hose can be attached.

INSULATION

Materials used in walls and ceilings to prevent heat from penetrating or escaping from ceilings or exterior walls.

LEACHING LINES

Part of a leach system consisting of a series of perforated pipes which allow the effluent from a septic tank to leach into the soil.

LOT BOUNDARY LINE

The line around the perimeter of a piece of property that indicates the legal boundary. This line is usually established by a surveyor.

MASONRY

Stone, brick, block, tiles, or concrete, used to form the walls or other parts of a structure.

MECHANICAL PENCIL

A pencil made especially for drafting consisting of a metal or plastic holder into which separate leads are inserted. Leads of various grades are interchangeable in this type of pencil.

MOLDING

Decoratively shaped trim, usually of wood, used to finish joints such as those in wall finishes at the ceiling line or to trim openings such as doors, windows, etc.

NORTH ARROW

An arrow drawn on a plot plan to indicate the direction of north.

OPAQUE PAPER
Paper you cannot see pencil lines through when tracing.

ORIENTATION
The way the house is placed on the lot in relationship to the sun.

OVERHANG
That portion of the roof, second story, or deck that projects beyond the exterior walls.

OVERLAY
Translucent tracing paper laid over a drawing for the purpose of revising the first drawing.

PLOT PLAN
A plan of a lot showing the existing features and the proposed new construction.

PRELIMINARY FLOOR PLAN
A sketch representing first ideas for the arrangement of rooms and the shape of a house.

ROOF PITCH
The rise or slope of a roof.

ROUGH-IN PLUMBING
Permanent, concealed parts of piping, usually in the framed wall.

RUNNING BOND
A masonry pattern, also called 1/2 bond.

SCALE
A line length used to represent a unit of measure (as a quarter of an inch to a foot). Also a measuring instrument.

SCHEMATIC DIAGRAM
A planning diagram.

SERVICE AREA
An area, on a lot, set aside for work space and equipment used in maintenance, gardening, or other tasks.

SETBACK
Space requirements regarding the placement of a house on a lot. City or county planning departments usually require that houses be set back from the lot boundary lines a certain distance. These requirements vary and must be verified with local planning or building departments.

SOLID-CORE DOOR
A door with a core that is solid as opposed to one that is hollow.

SPECIFICATIONS
Description of materials, equipment, construction methods, standards, and workmanship requirements. Included as part of the plans and the construction contract.

SQUARE FOOTAGE
A unit of measurement used to define the floor area of a house.

STACKED BOND
A masonry pattern.

SUBDIVISION MAP
A map of the subdivision in which subject property is located. Usually prepared by the developer and approved by city or county planners.

TRAFFIC PATHS
The paths through the house where people are most apt to walk from one area or room to another.

VELLUM
Translucent paper suitable for drafting purposes.

WALLBOARD
Wall finishing material, usually of gypsum or wood paneling that is nailed to framing studs and finished in a variety of ways.

WEATHERSTRIP
Metal, rubber, vinyl, or fabric used around doors and windows to make them as airtight as possible.

WHITEPRINTING
A method of making prints from original translucent drawings.

WINDOW SASH
The wood or metal surrounding the glass in any type of window.

WING
A part of a building extending out from the main structure.

GLOSSARY OF BUILDING INDUSTRY CAREERS

DESIGN PROFESSIONALS

ARCHITECT

A registered architect is one who has completed architectural studies in college and has served an apprenticeship, usually in the office of an architect. The architectural candidate is registered by the state upon completion of an examination given by the State Board of Architectural Examiners of that state in which the candidate resides. In some states, candidates are permitted to take the examination when they have a prescribed number of years of actual experience.

The function of an architect is to design buildings and provide clients with plans and specifications.

REGISTERED BUILDING DESIGNER

In some states, designers who have had a prescribed number of years of practical experience in the field of building design are permitted to submit substantiating drawings and documents to the State Board of Architectural Examiners, along with an application for registration as a Building Designer. Those who are approved are issued certificates of registration as building designers.

The function of a building designer is to design buildings and provide clients with plans and specifications.

ARCHITECTURAL DRAFTERS

An architectural drafter is one who translates the architect's or building designer's design sketches into complete sets of working drawings. Drafters often serve as liaison between designer and

builder and sometimes between designer and client. With experience, study, and talent, some drafters become excellent designers and eventually work on their own, serving builders and/or clients directly.

Some states have procedures for licensing architectural drafters.

LANDSCAPE ARCHITECT

The work of the landscape architect is related to the building site, and may include orientation of the structure, earth work, layout of paved areas and landscaping. An extensive understanding of plant life is essential. The landscape architectural candidate must complete the required curriculum or have equivalent practical experience to become qualified to take the state examination and become registered.

STRUCTURAL ENGINEER

A structural engineer is usually a civil engineer specializing in structures. Architects and building designers usually engage structural engineers to work out stress calculations and sometimes to prepare drawings of certain structural details of buildings. The services of a structural engineer are rarely required for the design of uncomplicated one or two story buildings. The work of the structural engineer is performed primarily on plans for commercial and/or industrial buildings.

GENERAL CONTRACTOR

A general contractor is one who has been licensed by the state to contract with clients to build structures of various types. It is illegal for a person who is not a licensed contractor to enter into such a contract. A general contractor is qualified, through education and practical experience, to analyze plans drawn by others, estimate the cost to construct the building(s), and to perform any other work pertaining to the project. The general contractor obtains building permits, hires qualified craftspersons (usually called subcontractors) in each of the respective crafts to perform the actual work. He or she coordinates and overseas the work, calls for inspections and deals with inspectors, handles and distributes the construction funds, and is responsible for the ultimate completion of all phases of the project, in accordance with approved plans and specifications, according to the terms and conditions of the contract agreement.

SUBCONTRACTOR

A subcontractor is one who is licensed to perform one or more of the many crafts in the building industry. There are subcontractors in the field of framing, electrical wiring, plumbing, painting, to mention only a few.

To become a subcontractor, one might begin as an apprentice in the chosen craft and work up to journeyman. With considerable practical experience and often additional study, the qualified individual may make application to the state and take an examination to become a licensed subcontractor in his or her specific craft.

The licensed subcontractor is qualified to enter into a contractural agreement with a general contractor or with an owner/builder, to perform that portion of the work that he or she is licensed to do. The subcontractor sometimes obtains building permits for the portion of the work contracted for and must perform the work in such a way that it will pass inspection.

OWNER/BUILDER

An owner/builder is one who chooses to build his or her own home without benefit of a general contractor. Building permits are issued to those individuals who own land and present acceptable plans to the building department. Most building and planning department personnel are very helpful to owner/builders in clarifying requirements and explaining procedures and required changes.

The owner/builder usually contracts with individual subcontractors to perform the various construction crafts. An owner/builder, working without benefit of a general contractor, must perform all of the tasks mentioned above under the heading **General Contractor**.

JOURNEYMAN

A journeyman is a union member who has completed apprenticeship training and has been qualified as a journeyman, by the union of which he or she becomes a member, and has been issued a journeyman card in the respective craft.

APPRENTICE

An apprentice is a person who is being trained, both on the job and in the classroom, in his or her chosen craft.

205

PROJECT LIST

Materials Required: *Design guides and 1/4-in. scale ruler from Pages 215 through 229, squared drawing paper*

For a new home or an addition: Your preliminary plan, notes, evaluation list, list of furniture measurements, small sheets of tracing paper, pencil, eraser, colored pencil, drafting tape

For remodeling or rearranging: A 1/4-in. scale drawing of each room you plan to revise drawn on squared drawing paper, a list of sizes of each piece of furniture or equipment to be used in each room, small tracing paper, pencil, eraser, colored pencil, drafting tape

—CHAPTER EIGHT—
PLANNING VEHICLE AREAS

Things To Consider When Planning A Garage Or Carport

Objective: *To plan a garage so that maximum use is made of the available space. This can be achieved by carefully planning the placement of doors, windows, parking-space allowances, and other facilities.*

Materials Required: *A 1/4-in. scale ruler, design guides, squared drawing paper, your preliminary garage plan, list of items the garage must accommodate and the size of each, pencil, eraser, colored pencil, drafting tape*

—CHAPTER NINE—
DEVELOPING THE OVER-ALL PLAN

Converting Your Preliminary Floor Plan To A Working Drawing

Objective: *To draw a final plan from which the house can be built.*

Materials Required: *A 1/4-in. scale ruler, design guides, all your preliminary drawings, sketches, lists, large sheets of squared drawing paper, tracing paper of equal size, pencils, eraser, colored pencil, drafting tape*

How To Convey Actual Size Information

Objective: *To learn a simple method of indicating actual sizes on your floor-plan drawing.*

Materials Required: *A 1/4-in. scale ruler, your plan, a well-pointed pencil with a hard lead for drawing dimension lines, a pencil with a softer lead for writing figures, drafting tape, (a triangle would be very useful for drawing long dimension and extension lines, see Fig. 8, Item F)*

How To Convey Special Information

Objective: *To learn how special information can be added to the plan.*

Materials Required: *Straight edge for ruling guide lines, your floor plan, pencil, eraser, drafting tape*

Changes And How To Make Them

Objective: *To learn how to handle suggestions for changes in the plan made by subcontractors and others and to make them on the drawings.*

Materials Required: *A 1/4-in. scale ruler, design guides, your floor plan, tracing paper, pencils, eraser, colored pencil*

How To Draw A Final Plot Plan

Objective: *To draw a plan of the lot showing the placement of the house and enough other information to acquaint workers with the project requirements.*

Materials Required: *The 1/16-in. scale ruler from Page 229, a small sheet of squared drawing paper, your original plot plan drawing, sketches and notes, tracing paper, pencil, eraser, colored pencil, drafting tape*

INDEX

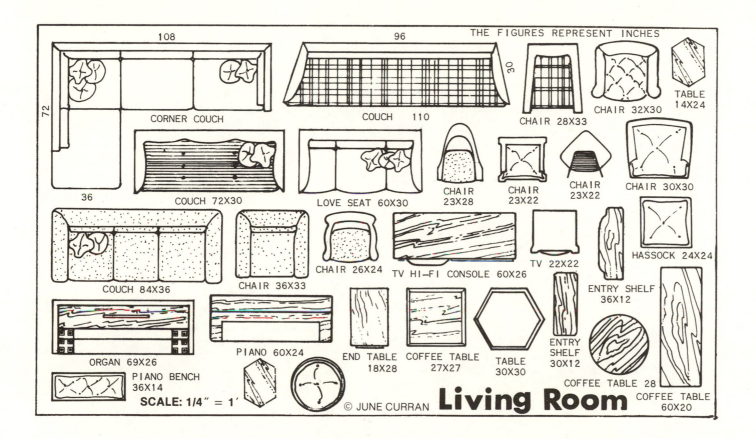

THE FIGURES REPRESENT INCHES

108

96

72

30

CORNER COUCH

36

COUCH 110

CHAIR 32X30

CHAIR 28X33

TABLE 14X24

COUCH 72X30

LOVE SEAT 60X30

CHAIR 23X28

CHAIR 23X22

CHAIR 23X22

CHAIR 30X30

COUCH 84X36

CHAIR 36X33

CHAIR 26X24

TV HI-FI CONSOLE 60X26

TV 22X22

HASSOCK 24X24

ENTRY SHELF 36X12

ORGAN 69X26

PIANO 60X24

END TABLE 18X28

COFFEE TABLE 27X27

TABLE 30X30

ENTRY SHELF 30X12

PIANO BENCH 36X14

SCALE: 1/4" = 1'

© JUNE CURRAN

COFFEE TABLE 28

COFFEE TABLE 60X20

Living Room

215

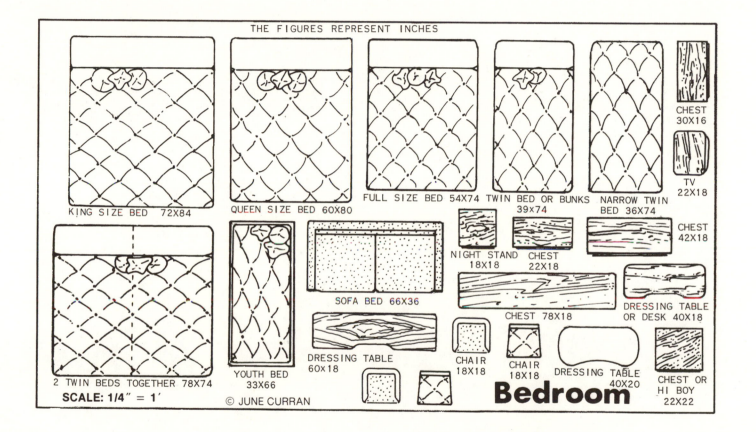

THE FIGURES REPRESENT INCHES

KING SIZE BED 72X84

QUEEN SIZE BED 60X80

FULL SIZE BED 54X74

TWIN BED OR BUNKS 39x74

NARROW TWIN BED 36X74

CHEST 30X16

TV 22X18

CHEST 42X18

NIGHT STAND 18X18

CHEST 22X18

CHEST 78X18

DRESSING TABLE OR DESK 40X18

2 TWIN BEDS TOGETHER 78X74

SCALE: 1/4" = 1'

YOUTH BED 33X66

© JUNE CURRAN

SOFA BED 66X36

DRESSING TABLE 60x18

CHAIR 18X18

CHAIR 18X18

DRESSING TABLE 40X20

Bedroom

CHEST OR HI BOY 22X22

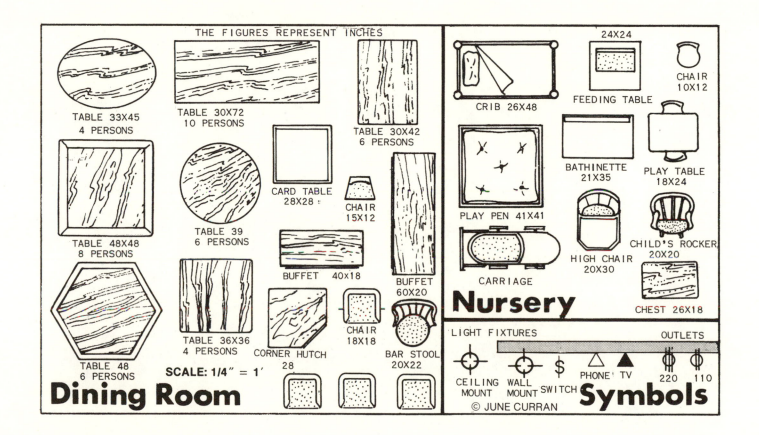

THE FIGURES REPRESENT INCHES

TABLE 33X45
4 PERSONS

TABLE 30X72
10 PERSONS

TABLE 30X42
6 PERSONS

TABLE 48X48
8 PERSONS

TABLE 39
6 PERSONS

CARD TABLE
28X28

CHAIR
15X12

BUFFET 40x18

BUFFET
60X20

TABLE 48
6 PERSONS

TABLE 36X36
4 PERSONS

CORNER HUTCH
28

CHAIR
18X18

BAR STOOL
20X22

SCALE: 1/4″ = 1′

Dining Room

CRIB 26X48

FEEDING TABLE

24X24

CHAIR
10X12

BATHINETTE
21X35

PLAY TABLE
18X24

PLAY PEN 41X41

HIGH CHAIR
20X30

CHILD'S ROCKER
20X20

CARRIAGE

CHEST 26X18

Nursery

LIGHT FIXTURES   OUTLETS

CEILING
MOUNT

WALL
MOUNT

$ SWITCH

PHONE TV

220   110

© JUNE CURRAN

Symbols

219

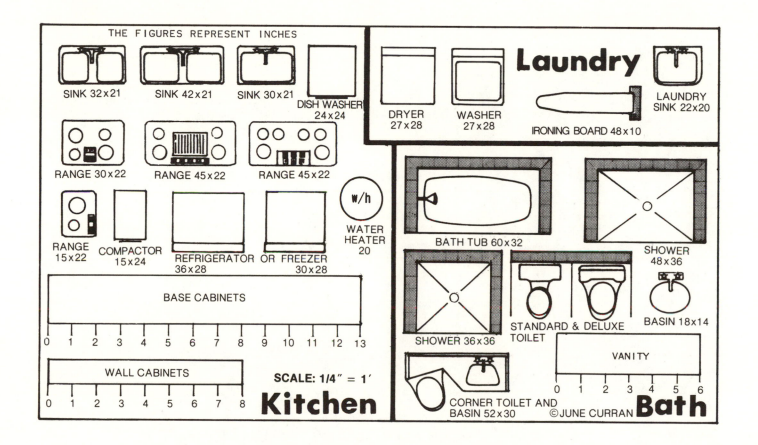

THE FIGURES REPRESENT INCHES

SINK 32 x 21

SINK 42 x 21

SINK 30 x 21

DISH WASHER
24 x 24

RANGE 30 x 22

RANGE 45 x 22

RANGE 45 x 22

RANGE
15 x 22

COMPACTOR
15 x 24

REFRIGERATOR
36 x 28

OR FREEZER
30 x 28

w/h
WATER
HEATER
20

BASE CABINETS

0 1 2 3 4 5 6 7 8 9 10 11 12 13

WALL CABINETS

0 1 2 3 4 5 6 7 8

SCALE: 1/4″ = 1′

Kitchen

Laundry

DRYER
27 x 28

WASHER
27 x 28

IRONING BOARD 48 x 10

LAUNDRY
SINK 22 x 20

BATH TUB 60 x 32

SHOWER
48 x 36

SHOWER 36 x 36

STANDARD & DELUXE
TOILET

BASIN 18 x 14

VANITY

0 1 2 3 4 5 6

CORNER TOILET AND
BASIN 52 x 30

©JUNE CURRAN **Bath**

THE FIGURES REPRESENT INCHES

1 MASONRY FIREPLACE FRONT OPENING 36 HEARTH 18

2 MASONRY CORNER FIREPLACE OPEN 2 SIDES 42 AND 30 HEARTH 18

3 MASONRY FIREPLACE OPENING 2 SIDES 40 HEARTH 2 SIDES 18

4 MASONRY FIREPLACE OPEN 3 SIDES 36 AND 24 HEARTH 18 3 SIDES

5 FREE—STANDING FIREPLACE HEARTH 48X48

6 FREE—STANDING FIREPLACE HEARTH 46X46

Fireplaces

SCALE: 1/4″ = 1′

PORTABLE BARBECUE 30

CHAISE LOUNGE 36X72

HAMMOCK 26X68

TABLE AND BENCHES 38X68

SERVING CART 16X54

CHAIR 20X18

TABLE 16

CHAIR 20X30

CHAIR 20X20

CHAIR 23X22

© JUNE CURRAN

Patio

223

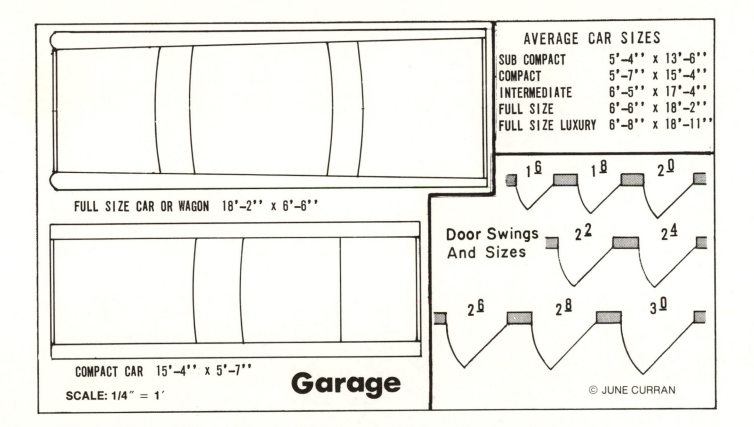

FULL SIZE CAR OR WAGON   18'–2'' x 6'–6''

COMPACT CAR   15'–4'' x 5'–7''

SCALE: 1/4" = 1'

Garage

AVERAGE CAR SIZES

SUB COMPACT	5'–4'' x 13'–6''
COMPACT	5'–7'' x 15'–4''
INTERMEDIATE	6'–5'' x 17'–4''
FULL SIZE	6'–6'' x 18'–2''
FULL SIZE LUXURY	6'–8'' x 18'–11''

Door Swings And Sizes

16   18   20

22   24

26   28   30

© JUNE CURRAN

225

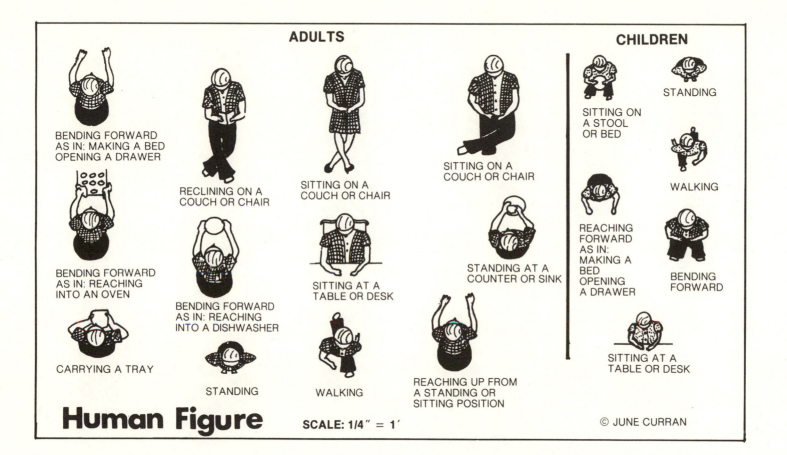

ADULTS

CHILDREN

BENDING FORWARD AS IN: MAKING A BED OPENING A DRAWER

RECLINING ON A COUCH OR CHAIR

SITTING ON A COUCH OR CHAIR

SITTING ON A COUCH OR CHAIR

SITTING ON A STOOL OR BED

STANDING

BENDING FORWARD AS IN: REACHING INTO AN OVEN

BENDING FORWARD AS IN: REACHING INTO A DISHWASHER

SITTING AT A TABLE OR DESK

STANDING AT A COUNTER OR SINK

REACHING FORWARD AS IN: MAKING A BED OPENING A DRAWER

WALKING

BENDING FORWARD

CARRYING A TRAY

STANDING

WALKING

REACHING UP FROM A STANDING OR SITTING POSITION

SITTING AT A TABLE OR DESK

Human Figure

SCALE: 1/4″ = 1′

© JUNE CURRAN

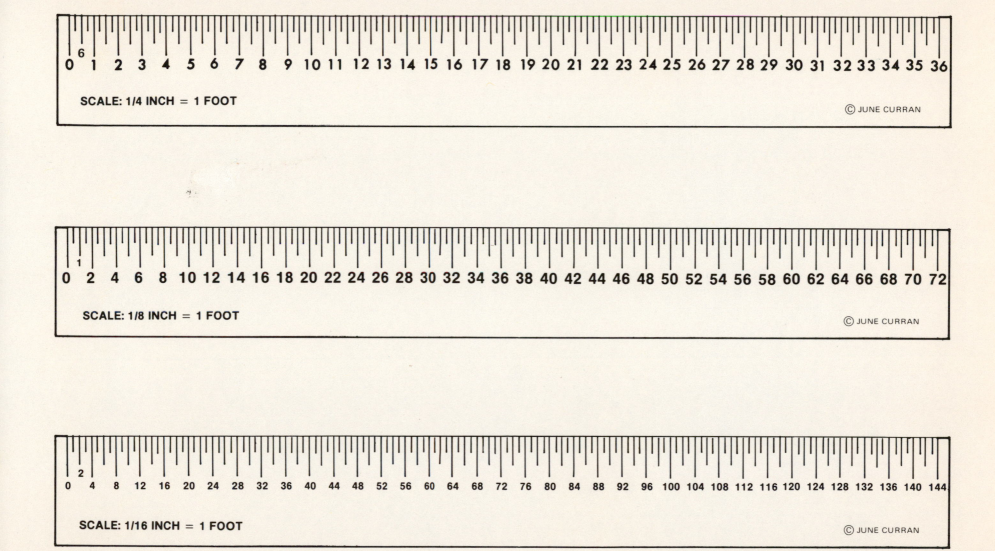

SCALE: 1/4 INCH = 1 FOOT

© JUNE CURRAN

SCALE: 1/8 INCH = 1 FOOT

© JUNE CURRAN

SCALE: 1/16 INCH = 1 FOOT

© JUNE CURRAN